PUBLIC GOOD
AND POLITICAL AUTHORITY

Kennikat Press
National University Publications
Series in American Studies

General Editor
James P. Shenton
Professor of History, Columbia University

WILLIAM J. MEYER

PUBLIC GOOD
AND
POLITICAL AUTHORITY

A Pragmatic Proposal

National University Publications
KENNIKAT PRESS • 1975
Port Washington, N.Y. • London

Manufactured in the United States of America

Published by
Kennikat Press Corp.
Port Washington, N.Y./London

Library of Congress Cataloging in Publication Data

Meyer, William J
    Public good and political authority.

    (National university publications)
    Bibliography: p.
    Includes index.
    1. Public interest.   2. Authority.   I. Title.
JC507.M53   301.5'92   75-29438
ISBN 0-8046-9112-6

CONTENTS

To Joan, Rachel, and Hannah

PREFACE

Several years ago Bertrand de Jouvenel called political science the study of "public authorities," but the task he identified hardly represents the actual tradition of inquiry that has developed in the discipline. The idea of the "public" has been reduced to legalistic and formalistic terms and it has become quite common to reject the notion that the public could be a concrete human group that may plausibly be said to have an "interest." The treatment of the concept of authority is even more serious, for that vital political idea around which so much of western political thought has grown has come to connote little more than the stem of "authoritarianism." Whatever the actual details of the cause-effect relationship, the increased desire for a more systematic and scientific treatment of politics seems to have led to a less conscious shift in focus from *auctoritas* to *potestas,* from power as acknowledged authority to power as force. If all political systems are, at their root, systems of authority, we should rightly question why so little political analysis seems to derive from a concern for the dynamics involved in establishing, augmenting, changing, reshaping, and challenging public authority. The tradition of "realistic" social science has tended to obscure these processes by passing off public appeals to legitimacy as illusions and superstitions (Gaetano Mosca), "soul stuff" (Arthur Bentley), or, more recently, personal moralism (Lewis Froman and John Bunzel). Yet this disparagement of the function of authoritative political ideas, whether they consist of liberal constitutionalism, Marxist-Leninism, Divine Right, or whatever, is itself unrealistic in light of the necessity for such ideas, the vital role they perform in political stability and change, and the fundamental desire of men to know whether the direction of their public life is right and to feel confident in that knowledge.

With this in mind, the purpose of the following study may be identified, first, by making clear what it is not intended to be. It is not intended to be primarily a contribution to the literature of pragmatic philosophy; nor is it intended to be primarily a critique of American pluralist writing. Rather, the study takes off from both of these points; that is, it takes critiques of pluralism as part of the context of recent political inquiry calling for the exploration of new modes of analysis and new paradigms, and it takes pragmatism, in a pragmatic spirit, as an approach to the study of man to be used and applied in seeking such an alternative. The primary purpose of the study is to construct a usable conception of the public interest, and to suggest how this concept may be the focal point of new analytical approaches that may return political inquiry to the task of understanding the workings of public authority. There will be little discussion of all the various historical interpretations of the public interest and related ideas such as "the common good" or "collective will." One reason for this is that surveys and categorizations of what the term means have already been done by people like Glendon Schubert, Richard Flathman and Virginia Held. Another reason is that much criticizing of classical conceptions of the public interest has been done and what is really needed at this point is a positive attempt to explore theoretically the usefulness of the concept. Thus, what this study represents is not an examination of a political theory or theories; rather, it is intended as itself an exercise in theorizing, directed toward the clarification of an important concept for the purpose of making that concept a useful focus for political analysis. It takes off from what is presented as the state of the literature on the public interest, which is generally diffuse and inconclusive as far as it concerns any positive function for the concept in political analysis, and though this investigation necessarily touches upon numerous issues in political theory, thorough treatment is only claimed for the specific task that has been identified. The contribution of this effort should be measurable, if not quantifiable: can we better understand what is happening in a political system by including in our analysis some explanation of the performance of the system in regard to effective identification and pursuit of the public interest?

The idea of the public interest may seem an unpromising point around which to develop a new framework of analysis. Yet the use of the idea is appealing, for while it has been commonly rejected in the search for rigorous analytical and empirical approaches to inquiry and while it conveys no settled-upon meaning, it still raises to our attention very concrete, though unwieldy, dilemmas in the establishment and maintenance of political order. While we dismiss the public interest as anything "real," we find that political experience continually confronts us with a sense of the "publicness" of political acts, with a common and shared fate, with the evidence that beyond the scope of our own lives and personal interests there is a public condition of affairs created, directly or indirectly, consciously or unconsciously, by men in association with one another. If we are really to understand the full range of political phenomena, we must consider the extent to which such a "public condition" operates as the object of human control, power, value, and belief.

It should be confessed that the author takes no small amount of enjoyment in the fact that the wide variety of people who have looked at the manuscript have experienced considerable frustration in pinning an ideological label on the position that is taken. Behind this confusion there lies a curious mentality which seems to assume that if you merely speak about the public interest you are a romantic, if you speak about authority you are a conservative, if you speak about the concrete payoffs of public policy you are utilitarian. Perhaps the record can be set straight quickly by reporting that the book speaks of all these things and the author is a democrat. Yet the book deals with political theory and one of its fundamental assumptions is that concern with such things as authority, the public interest, and policy payoffs should not be viewed as the private preserve of particular ideological schools.

The book is essentially divided into three parts. The first part (Chapters 1-4) identifies the context of the problem and shows how the question of what the public interest is is analytically and empirically meaningful and important. The second part (Chapters 5-8) introduces the pragmatic approach with a view to its merits over conventional functionalist and operationalist thinking, especially in regard to the problem of values. The third part (Chapters 9-11) applies pragmatism to the unique problem of the public interest and suggests how it may be used as a focal point for analyzing political stability and change.

Among all of the people who aided so much in this project I would like to take this opportunity to thank specifically Eldon Eisenach and John Wikse for their perceptive and valuable criticisms.

CHAPTER ONE

THE ECLIPSE
OF THE PUBLIC INTEREST

At the heart of many difficulties of American politics there lies a critical and unresolved problem of American political thought. This problem is that the pervasively liberal tradition in America has not been able to account satisfactorily for political language and political acts that fall outside a limited view of individual and private group interests. The classical problem of the common good or the public interest is doubly problematic when placed within a liberal setting where the public realm is naturally viewed with suspicion. The observation that the liberal ideology of American politics does not include any substantial view of the public interest is, in fact, one of the few points of agreement among writers of very different persuasions about the value of liberalism itself.[1] But the problem also operates on another level; it has a whole other dimension. Not only does American public life suffer under the suspicions of a liberal fear of authority and collective purpose, but political science has also waged its own attack. The weapon at the hand of theory is the control of language and the public interest has been dealt the most critical blow of being designated "meaningless." Thus, the idea of the public interest is not only unimportant to the workings of liberal politics, it is also unimportant to political theory. The concern here is whether either of these situations is justifiable.

Though the real meaning of the public interest—involving common purposes, shared goals, etc.—has little credibility today,

3

the term is sometimes kept in use and given other kinds of meanings. It is not uncommon today to salvage the term "public interest" for certain analytical uses. The term and the manner in which it and its synonyms are employed are themselves part of the data of experience; they perform a hortatory function in politics. People appeal to the public interest as a justification for political action; they claim to act by its dictates and on this basis encourage others to follow.[2] Though David Truman claims that "we do not need to account for a totally inclusive interest, because one does not exist," he nevertheless describes the manner in which appeals to such an inclusive interest are normally used for propaganda purposes.[3] Such appeals, especially when framed in terms of national security, are emotionally and symbolically useful in mustering support and solidarity.[4] Frank Sorauf has noted the use of such public symbols for purposes of creating and sustaining widespread agreement, without necessarily contributing to the solution of policy questions.[5] Several decades ago Harold Lasswell saw that the public interest was a way of rationalizing the displacement of private motives onto public objects.[6] The analytical focus of these various views is not on the public interest as something with a specified content but on the fact of a claim or assertion of such an interest. The making of the claim is the event to be explained and it is explained in a functional or instrumental way. There are people who talk about the public interest, and that is a phenomenon worth looking into. This talk is interpreted to mean, not that there really is a public interest, but that apparently some political function is served by the talk itself, presumably an exhortative, symbolic function.

Another common adaptation of the term is the pluralist view that the public interest stands for either the political process itself or the outcome of the process, despite what that outcome might be. Glendon Schubert, in his thorough review of the literature on the matter, designates this "realist theory." He summarizes the realist position in this way:

The realists are skeptics and sophisticates who have put behind them myths which postulate any independent substantive content for such notions as "the public will" and "the public interest." For them, the alternatives for official choice are concrete but ambiguous. The supreme virtue of a democratic system of government is the multiplicity of points of access that it affords for the manifold conflicting interests which necessarily arise in a pluralistic society. The function of government officials is to facilitate the continuous readjustment of conflicting interests, with a minimum of disturbance of existing equilibria.[7]

As clearly stated by one such "realist," this simply means that "what may be called public policy is actually the equilibrium reached in the group struggle at any given moment."[8] Peter Odegard has argued that this position eliminates reason, knowledge and intelligence from the processes of governing and makes policy —to use a technical metaphor—the vector-sum of political forces.[9] Newton's laws of motion have replaced human will. Though this point of view may take many forms,[10] it suggests that the term be used to refer to processes and their mechanically explained outcomes. This may be an attempt to show how a classical term can be related to contemporary analytical categories, but through this salvage job the term is stripped of any of its distinctive significance. The use of the term in this way is often gratuitous.

Joseph Schumpeter concurs with the realists in their skepticism, though he might prefer to dismiss the notion of a public interest entirely rather than maintain the term as an empty shell. He argues quite unequivocally that "there is no such thing as a uniquely determined common good that all people could agree on or be made to agree on by the force of rational argument."[11] He is not prepared to impute a "common good" label to what results from democratic processes; indeed, he sees such imputation as a carry-over of classical democratic theory for which he has little sympathy. He continues:

But though a common will or public opinion of some sort may still be said to emerge from the infinitely complex jumble of individual and group-wise situations, volitions, influences, actions and reactions of the "democratic process," the result lacks not only rational unity but also rational sanction.[12]

According to this view, the utilitarian notion of an identity of interests, for example, is merely an attempt to "anoint the results that process turns out with oil taken from eighteenth century jars."[13] Schumpeter is quite candid in noting that "it is not only conceivable but, whenever individual wills are much divided, very likely that the political decisions produced will not conform to 'what people really want.' "[14] Visions of the common good can no longer be entertained; they are dangerous and unworkable. The liberal democracy that has evolved is quite satisfactory and desirable if taken very honestly for what it is, without pretense.

Two political scientists who have reviewed this whole question have affirmed Schumpeter's position. Glendon Schubert's inventory of the literature is thorough and detailed and his conclusions are worth quoting at length:

American writers in the field of political science have evolved neither a unified nor a consistent theory to describe how the public interest is defined in governmental decision-making; they have not constructed theoretical models with the degree of precision and specificity necessary if such models are to be used as descriptions of, or as a guide to, the actual behavior of real people. A theory of the public interest in governmental decision-making ought to describe a relationship between concepts of the public interest and official behavior in such terms that it might be possible to attempt to validate empirically hypotheses concerning the relationship. If extant theory does not lend itself to such uses, it is difficult to comprehend the justification for teaching students of political science that subservience to the public interest is a relevant norm of official responsibility.

Moreover, our investigation has failed to reveal a statement of public-interest theory that offers much promise either as a guide to public officials who are supposed to make decisions in the public interest, or to research scholars who might wish to investigate the extent to which governmental decisions are empirically made in the public interest. For either of the latter purposes, it would be necessary to have operational definitions of the public-interest concept; and neither my analysis nor that of other contemporary critics suggests that the public-interest theory prevalent in America today either is operational or is readily capable of being made operational.[15]

In the final analysis, despite the compromising uses of the term suggested by pluralists, Schubert concludes that

if the public-interest concept makes no operational sense, notwithstanding the efforts of a generation of capable scholars, then political scientists might better spend their time nurturing concepts that offer greater promise of becoming useful tools in the scientific study of political responsibility.[16]

Frank Sorauf concurs in the view that "the term is too burdened with multiple meanings for valuable use as a tool of political analysis."[17] In addition, Sorauf states that

perhaps academicians ought to take the lead in drawing up a list of ambiguous words and phrases "which never would be missed." For such a list I would have several candidates, but it should suffice here to nominate the "public interest."[18]

These, of course, are the considered views of two political scientists who have surveyed, analyzed, condensed, and summarized the dominant views regarding the public interest. Their conclusion is that the notion of a substantial public interest is not very useful in formal political analysis.

The "public interest" appears to be treated in many different ways, but the variety is quite spurious.[19] All of the above treatments reflect an attempt to formulate an operational concept consistent with the methods of empirical science. As such, they fall into two categories: the term is made operational or it is rejected as illusory and unreal because it cannot be made operational. In the former case, the concept "public interest" is identified in terms of its functional relation to real politics; it is the "equilibrium at any given moment" or a stock "rhetorical device" used by the politician. The concept refers immediately to certain actions, processes, and operations. What particular equilibrium might be reached or what particular rhetorical device might be in vogue is irrelevant to the concept; it is not part of the meaning of the public interest. In the latter case, to reject the concept outright as meaningless and unreal means that there is no chance that it "either is [operational] or is readily capable of being made operational."

The critical distinction at issue here is between the idea of a substantive interest of the public (classical view) and the operational meanings of the term "public interest" (contemporary view). Richard Flathman explains that "in most of its uses the noun 'interest' denotes a two-termed relationship between someone or something . . . and a substantive in which that person or thing 'has an interest.' "[20] The contemporary question of what the public interest means is couched in such a way as to make the "substantive" incidental and irrelevant. The "substantive" becomes problematic for political science because it encompasses questions of goals and values. When the public interest is taken to be meaningless, at the very least this refers to any conception of the public interest claiming an intelligible substantive referent. The relevance of this distinction to the eclipse of the public interest concept leads Flathman to argue that

the "abandon public interest" school of thought is not concerned with politics or justification at all, but with a more tender growth known as political science. Desiring to turn political science into a hard science on *their* model of the natural sciences, these writers wish to cut away all concepts, questions, and concerns which, in their view, hold political science back from this goal. *Political science* ought to eschew value judgments and cut away all concepts stricken with the cancer of ambiguity and imprecision generated by value judgments. If politicians, journalists, or citizens wish to concern themselves with the public interest, political science will not object. But the discipline itself must remain pure and exclude from its conceptual apparatus such prescientific curiosities.[21]

This calls to mind the recently increased criticism and reappraisal of functional, empirical, and operational modes of political analysis. Herbert Marcuse, for example, suggests a critical distinction between functional and operational concepts and cognitive concepts. In the operational use of language, "the 'thing identified with its function' is more real than the thing distinguished from its function," and such formulations "stand in the way of differentiation, separation and distinction," and "dissolve concepts in operations and exclude the conceptual intent which is opposed to such dissolution."[22] For Marcuse, the overall effect of this is the creation of a "one-dimensional universe of discourse and action" in which essential contradictions and negations seem to be wiped away or absorbed.[23] Indeed, the operationalist treatment of the public interest does seem to wipe away the historical struggles with which liberal thought had been confronted: the problem of universal and particular, individual and collective, Rousseau's general will standing in opposition to Bentham's sum of particular wills. The assertion of a public interest no longer stands as a possible threat to liberalism, since empirical science has offered the choice of treating the concept in its merely functional dimensions or else dismissing it with impunity. A vicious circle becomes completed with the assertion that any other form of conception, one that might stand in opposition and clarify contradictions, is unreal and meaningless because it does not refer to observable operations. That is, a concept only wins approval in social science once it is fully realized in the social world. The end result is the fact/value dichotomy in which "values separated out from the objective reality become subjective" and supra-empirical concepts "become mere ideals, and their concrete, critical content evaporates into the ethical or metaphysical atmosphere."[24] The concept "public interest" seems to be a victim of this style of thought.

Thus, to reopen the question of a substantive public good requires a reconsideration of empirical social science and its claims to objectivity, realism, and ideological neutrality. The relationship among philosophy, ideology, and empirical theory—and among facts, concepts, and values—has increasingly been seen as quite problematic. Typical of this revisionism are the charges that empirical models contain built-in ideological biases, that a scientific view of the world itself rests on root values not demonstrable in scientific terms, and that concepts may be real and empirically objective in some non-operational sense.[25] The ensuing debate is relevant because the public interest concept, like many basic concepts in political science, has been subjected to empirical-behavioral attempts to "clarify" its meaning. The present flurry of revisionism, by going beyond mere technical criticism of method, suggests the possibility of substantial rethinking about the meaning of basic political concepts. Though the present inquiry is sympathetic to this revisionism, its goal will not be to add yet another systematic critique of empirical social science. Rather, the purpose is to do what must be done to make such criticism complete and whole—that is, to offer an alternate conception of a fundamental political term that better aids our understanding of political phenomena than existing conceptualizations.

The term "public interest" has much to recommend it as a pivot for such an inquiry. Through association with Aristotle's "good life" or Rousseau's "general will," the term carries with it the philosophical baggage of a long tradition of discourse that sought out the meaning of the social good. That is one side of the term; for present day political scientists, it is its antediluvian side. They want to shake loose the philosophical, ideological, and normative weightiness of the term, trim it down to size, and find out what it "really" means. For some, like Schubert and Sorauf, the term is irredeemable; for others it survives the translation into operational language. The term is thus a case in point of the metamorphosis of language in the behavioral revolution, and the new revisionism suggests the need for a critical examination of that essential change. The present inquiry assumes that in the process of convoluting or rejecting the concept of the public interest, something valuable was lost and that loss has served to shrink a tradition of discourse that contributed invaluably to the greater understanding of politics.

The operational language of social science is, of course, not without significance and its very positivistic form has surely caught vital facts in its net of meaning. One issue is whether or not politics actually reflects a concern with the public interest, with all of its classical connotations. On this score, pluralists and their critics have both observed and recorded the eclipse of the public interest in the American political system. This eclipse can be seen as consistent with the larger picture of American-style democracy. It is a situation that grows naturally from the soil of individualism, fear of the state and of authority, and the political defense of minorities. H. Mark Roelofs, in cogently summarizing these relationships, has noted that

liberal democrats, although appearing in the most determined manner to throw the discussion open to all comers, tacitly assume that the proper subjects for debate and negotiation are the welfare and opportunities, the *interests,* of particular individuals and groups. Talk about the "common good," when attempted, proves awkward and regularly gets twisted into phrases like "What's good for the country is good for General Motors, . . ."[26]

and:

Stress on the individual and hostility to the state are also the source of liberal democracy's most obvious weakness: In its vocabulary for political talk, it has hardly any conception of society as an organic whole at all.[27]

As the often-used analogy of the marketplace indicates, the expectation of liberal democracy has been that political institutions, like economics, could become neutral instruments, mechanisms designed to hold together the competitive wants, desires, and motivations of private men. In such a setting, a distinct direction and purpose for the state is, to say the least, problematic. In fact, Daniel Boorstin, in a flattering appraisal of American liberalism, contends that the very genius of such a system consists of its ability to avoid the social blueprints, planning, romantic ideology, and idolatry that characterize "our sick friends in Europe."[28] Private interests are seen as intelligible, primary, real units of politics; the public is at best a fictional composite of diverse elements and surely has no interest of its own. Political science has helped to identify and highlight the atrophy of the public interest idea in the political experience of America.

The feeling of immediate correspondence between observed fact and proposition gives a sense of positive validity to the empiricist's portrayal of American pluralism and leads to the suspicion that the theoretical critiques must be at root merely "normative" or "valuational." But is this all? Does concern with the public interest close with this description of its eclipse? Sheldon Wolin has described what Schubert's realists have gone through in rejecting the public interest:

The concept of anomaly suggests that a scientific crisis occurs because something is wrong "in" the theory. When nature does not conform to the scientist's expectations, he reacts by re-examining his techniques and theories. He assumes that the "mistake" lies with one or the other, not with nature.[29]

In this sense theory becomes a reflection of reality, more or less finely tuned to accurate focus. For the realists, the classical concern with the common good clearly had become an anomaly; in the real world of politics this anachronistic element made political theory look naive. The fuel of liberal politics was not common purpose but private ends and theory had to recognize, indeed internalize, this fact. In this sense, realist "theory" has proved to be quite sound and acceptable. The realist has offered a very good sketch of the condition of the public interest idea in the real political world, but rather than resolving any theoretical problems, this should begin to put theoretical problems into focus. How are we to make sense out of and judge the significance of the actual political eclipse of the public interest? A few preliminary observations about social theory and social concepts ought to suggest why it is important to go beyond the position of the realists.

One distinguishing mark of theories of man and society as opposed to theories of natural phenomena is that social theories have as their subject thinking beings. Social theory, therefore, does not go completely outside of itself to an external subject but turns in upon itself insofar as it is, to put it one way, thought about thought. In the physical sciences there is only one level of meaning, that of the scientist. In social theory there are two levels of meaning, that of the scientist and that of the subject, because the subject is of the same nature as the scientist, a thinking being who makes and communicates meanings to phenomena. It would not be improper to characterize social theory as the activity of theorists studying theorists. More commonly, this is thought of as a problem of subjectivity or bias, as Teilhard de Chardin has put it:

Subjectively, first of all, we are inevitably the focus of our own observation . . . [scientists] are now coming to realize that even the most objective of their observations are steeped in the conventions they adopted at the outset and by forms or habits of thought developed in the course of their research; so that, when they reach the end of their analyses they cannot tell with any certainty whether the structure they have made is the essence of the matter they are studying, or the reflection of their own thought.[30]

Exactly what is empirical theory putting into focus, the observed events or the events of the observer? As Chardin explains more vividly, "It is tiresome and even humbling for the observer to be thus fettered, to be obliged to carry with him everywhere the centre of the landscape he is crossing."[31] All sciences, including the physical sciences, are rooted in *Weltanschauungen,* but social science not only has a "world-view" but is involved in the study of "world-views" in action. Thus, there are the two levels of meaning in political science: ideology and political theory. Ideology is the set of meanings that are found in the point of view of the political actor *qua* actor; political theory represents the set of meanings of the political theorist interpreting and systematizing his data about the events of politics and the behavior of political men.

At stake is the relation between these two levels of meaning in social science, what might be called theoretical ideas versus ideas-in-use as defined by political actors. In the case of a realist "theory" of the public interest, what seems to have happened is that the political scientist, in accumulating the data of political life, has included prevailing ideas-in-use as conceptualizations of the data. The meaning given to phenomena by the actor comes to be the exclusive theoretical meaning, because it is the only one that is operational (because it is in operation?). The observation that liberal politics has been able to do without the notion of a public interest, at least in its classical sense, has been well established empirically by group theorists. It is an empirical fragment in the study of the politician's ideology, a statement describing what the term "the public interest" means to this person, the politician. But why should it mean the same thing to anyone else, specifically the observer/ theorist? If it is somehow argued that it should, then does it follow that ideas-in-use are to be automatically translated into theoretical ideas? Is the political theorist then simply a recorder or systematizer of the politician's own theory-in-use? How then would one distinguish political theory from ideology? The point is that when one has identified the unconcern with the public interest in the workings of American politics, that observation does not represent the end of inquiry into the matter; indeed, it represents the very beginning of the theorist's inquiry. What is the significance of this eclipse of the public interest? Why do political men see the public interest in this particular way? What is the effect of this situation on the character of their political life? What are the consequences for such issues as the basis of authority and the role of the citizen resulting from this political disparagement of the public interest?

In addition to the observation about the two levels of meaning in social theory, invoking operational criteria for the concept of the public interest also raises some important questions. A good example of the conceptual confusions that can result from operationalism as it is understood in today's social science is found in a recent discussion of the concept of "political equality" by Charles Cnudde and Deane Neubauer. The authors attempt to explain why the concept is difficult to operationalize:

The concept . . . has no literal empirical referent for the simple reason that no political organization of any significant size is capable of achieving full political equality. . . . Operationally, then, it can be a quite literally "meaningless" concept because it has no empirical referent.[32]

Though the authors do end up discovering ways in which the term is useful, the above explanation is still quite curious. In trying to show that the term lacks an empirical referent they actually allude to such a referent—the existence of political *in*equality. Is there not some operational connection between the positive and the negative, between what is known and unknown through direct observation? Are the authors doing anything more than brooding over whether the glass is half full or half empty? Is this example analogous to Truman's assertion that we need not account for all-inclusive interest because the world does not provide us with one? Is Truman offering us sufficient grounds to say, along with Sorauf, that the term will not be missed or, with Schubert, that it might well be ignored?

In order to deal with the theoretical questions raised about the public interest, it is necessary to explore valid meanings the concept may have beyond meanings it acquires through use by political actors; that is, beyond any meaning "given by the data." Theory may then be equipped to take on the critical role alluded to by Wolin. The lack of a public interest in the American polity is now accompanied by the lack of a critical theoretical standpoint from which to examine this phenomenon. The problem at this point is so fundamental that, as Virginia Held suggests, "before any proposal concerning the meaning of the public interest deserves a serious hearing, it may be necessary to answer the claim that the concept can simply be disposed of, done away with, ignored, or made extinct."[33] For this reason, before showing how the question of what the public interest is may be answerable, it will be necessary to address the more fundamental issue of why the question is significant. It would seem that this matter cannot be taken for granted.

Beyond a consideration of this point, the course of the argument to follow will lead us into two broad topics that will assist us in dealing with the central question. First, the issue of a belief in the idea of the public interest is closely intertwined with general epistemological questions of belief and knowledge. The question of the public interest is so tightly bound up with our view of social knowledge that it will be necessary to approach the central problem of the book by way of a digression into such broader concerns. Specifically, it will be argued that the central problems of the book can be usefully clarified and measurably resolved through an exploration of the applicability of the philosophic tradition of American pragmatism. Second, following upon the discussion of pragmatism, it will be argued that any consideration of the public interest will require an analysis of the function of legitimate public authority as the mode of articulating the public good. The questions of authority and of the public good will be seen to be closely wed.

It should be made clear at the outset that there is no intention to provide a historically or philosophically comprehensive review of the topic. The purpose is to attempt to make a specific case in a rather defined context: the case is that the question of the public interest is neither meaningless nor unanswerable, the context is the ideological and theoretical rejection of the public interest in America. Thus, the very framework of the book is pragmatic, for we are setting out to deal, not with all sorts of abstract and speculative doubts but, in the spirit of William James, with those live and concrete doubts that bound our political thinking.

Since, as has been noted, the eclipse of the public interest has gone beyond skepticism over the possibility of identifying what the public interest is and has included the assertion that the phrase itself and the problems it raises are meaningless and may be ignored, the first issue requiring attention is whether the term has an acceptable, empirically-based meaning and whether the problems it identifies are consequential for political man.

NOTES

Full bibliographic data for short form citations are given in Bibliography, beginning on page 142.

1. See Daniel Boorstin, Lewis Froman, John H. Bunzel, Mark Roelofs, and Robert Paul Wolff. All of these divergent and sometimes opposed interpretations of liberal politics in America commonly point, either approvingly or disapprovingly, to the eclipse of the public interest.
2. Wayne A. R. Leys, "The Relevance and Generality of the Public Interest," in Carl Friedrich and Murray Edelman, pp. 134–137.
3. David Truman, p. 51.
4. Truman, pp. 50, 358.
5. Frank Sorauf, p. 625.
6. Harold Lasswell, *Psychopathology and Politics*, pp. 75–76.
7. Glendon Schubert, p. 136.
8. Earl Latham, p. 390.
9. Peter Odegard, p. 699.
10. See, for example, Darryl Baskin, pp. 79–89; and Kirk Thompson, pp. 655–681.
11. Joseph Schumpeter, p. 251.
12. Schumpeter, p. 253.
13. Schumpeter, p. 253.
14. Schumpeter, p. 254.
15. Schubert, p. 220.
16. Schubert, p. 224.
17. Sorauf, p. 328.
18. Sorauf, "The Conceptual Muddle," in Friedrich, p. 190.
19. A handy summary of the various treatments given the public interest concept in the recent literature of political science can be found in the appendix to Virginia Held's book, pp. 223–226.
20. Richard Flathman, pp. 15–16.
21. Flathman, p. 83.
22. Herbert Marcuse, pp. 94–95.
23. Marcuse, pp. 84–89.
24. Marcuse, pp. 147–148.
25. In Section A of the Epilogue to the Second Edition of *The Political System*, David Easton summarizes the critiques of social science that provide the basis for what he calls the "post-behavioral revolution." Following are some of the more prominent articles and books that have explored the limitations of empirical/behavioral social science: C. Wright Mills; Harold Lasswell, *The Future of Political Science;* Thomas Kuhn; Stephen Toulmin; Fred M. Frohock; Charles A. McCoy and John Playford; William E. Connolly; Henry S. Kariel, "Normative Theory," in Michael Hass and Henry S. Kariel; Sheldon S. Wolin; Norman Jacobson.
26. Mark Roelofs, p. 201.
27. Roelofs, p. 189.
28. Daniel Boorstin, p. 183.
29. Sheldon S. Wolin, p. 1079.
30. Teilhard de Chardin, p. 32.
31. de Chardin, p. 32.
32. Charles Cnudde and Deane Neubauer, p. 11.
33. Virginia Held, p. 9.

CHAPTER TWO

JAMES
AND THE WILL TO BELIEVE

In dealing with the issue of why political scientists ought not to abandon the idea of a substantive public interest, it will be argued that the import and significance of this idea cannot be determined by narrow operational criteria but by the very character of man's political life and the kinds of decision problems that man confronts. The argument will contend that political scientists ought to talk about the public interest not because political actors might use the term, but because political phenomena display certain features that can best be conceptualized and understood through use of the public interest idea. The term's significance thus derives from certain considerations about the political world and from the desire for fruitful inquiry into it. In the process of responding to the claims of the "abandon public interest" school, this chapter and the next will—through the aid of insights drawn from two American pragmatists, William James and John Dewey—establish a logical and empirical context within which the investigation will be able to proceed to the central issue: What is the public interest?

Included in the study of politics are larger issues of human belief, knowledge, behavior, and action. The study of political life is in one sense only a facet of the study of human life and the most general terms used by political scientists reflect this; "power," "influence," and "decision-making" are not uniquely political terms. But there is also something special about political life as reflected in its own unique terms, such as "sovereignty," "rights," or perhaps "public interest." The discussion of the "public interest" thus partakes of both the specificity and generality of the language of political inquiry; it will be argued that the term is distinctly political while, at the same time, it is rooted in larger observations about human conduct and the human condition. Indeed, in order to demonstrate the critical importance of the term, it will be necessary to investigate philosophical issues regarding man's intellectual and social life that are not political issues as such.

That discussion of the public interest assumes certain views about shared human belief and conduct in general is revealed by the question most commonly raised in the matter: Who is to say what the public interest is? Does not the public interest concern issues of belief and value that stubbornly resist reliable methods of proof? Would not the assertion of a particular value or set of values as the public interest in a world of diverse and unprovable values raise serious social problems? Could this assertion be the basis for arbitrary authority; would it violate the rights of those who disagree? But then, how do men ever come together to share a common culture, system of belief, or set of institutions? Can it happen, as a conscious act, or is it always foisted upon them by historical circumstances? Is there something more primal about private motivations and rationales for action? Does the human condition offer an unlimited choice between personal and social bases of conduct; can the latter be delimited by an act of will, as it were? In other words, to what extent is it legitimate to try to escape collective forms of conduct as opposed to confronting the problems that they raise?

The last issue is important here because the question, "Who is to say what the public interest is?" frequently is answered by the claim that "no one has to say (or can say, or should say)." This assumes that something is wrong with the question, i.e., the presumption that "*someone* has to say." The "no one" answer was a critical contribution to the development of American pluralism, for it suggested that the "who is to say" question did not include a real empirical problem of human belief and action and that the question could be nullified, that is, the question does not state a problem at all. There is also the further dimension to the "no one" answer that if "no one says," then there is nothing to be said, no public subject of discourse. Hence, there is the "vector sum" interpretation that includes no reference to the content of the public interest, only to its nominal occurrence; after appropriate conditions about democratic and representative processes are laid down, whatever results *is* the public interest. In general, then, the "no one" answer suggests that the concept of the public interest—including who determines it, and what it is—is avoidable, both ideologically and theoretically, and can be dismissed with impunity. This would indicate that the first issue at stake is not how to answer the basic question of the public interest—who is to say what it is?—but how and why the question identifies real and important problems, or to put it another way, why "no one" is an inadequate answer. It is important to understand why an answer to the question should preserve the substantial meaning of the public interest, rather than merely preserve its usage in a convoluted form (vector-sum view) or dismiss it entirely (Schubert and Sorauf).

It will be argued here that the problem of determining the public interest is, in a certain sense, inescapable because of certain features of social action that, for various reasons, American pluralism has found it possible to ignore. The inescapable character of the problem derives from aspects of the human condition that have been dramatically laid out in the writings of the American pragmatists. In his essay entitled "The Will to Believe," William James presents an example of the application of the pragmatic point of view and its consequences for one's view of truth, belief, and action. As indicated earlier, the argument does not deal with specifically political situations but with a more general context, yet after examining the argument it should become clear how James's philosophical position sheds light on the problem at hand. Though written prior to the full exposition of James's thought, this essay represents an intense synthesis of the varied ingredients of pragmatism; more specifically, the logic of the essay is valuable for an understanding of the idea of a "social good." James's purpose in the essay, originally given in lecture form, is the "justification *of* faith, a defense of our right to adopt a believing attitude in religious matters, in spite of the fact that our merely logical intellect may not have been coerced."[1] The very statement of purpose contains a critical distinction: in the attempt to get at truth, to make judgments about it, two sides of us are at work, one logical and intellectual, the other "passional." The former can be "coerced" by brute facts to the point where our passions can add little to, and certainly not resist, the intellect's firm grasp of things. Man's passional nature increasingly has come to be considered an inadequate basis for judgments about the truth of things. James rests much of the argument that follows on an understanding of the context in which men establish their beliefs about the real world. This consists of viewing "anything that may be proposed to our belief" as a *hypothesis* and "the decision between two hypotheses an *option.*"[2] Three distinctions can be used to identify the kind of option being presented.[3] First, an option can be *live* or *dead.* To be live, an option must "be among the mind's possibilities," it "makes some appeal, however small, to your belief." Liveness and deadness are "relations to the individual thinker" that are "measured by his willingness to act" and include some "believing tendency." Second, an option may be either *forced* or *avoidable,* depending on the possibility of indifference to the choice; this means that a forced option is a "dilemma based on a complete logical disjunction." For James such a forced option would be presented by saying, "Either accept this truth or go without it." Finally, an option can be either *momentous* or *trivial,* the former being the case when the opportunity is unique and significant and the decision about it irreversible. Hesitation over a momentous option means the very option itself will pass by, which, in effect, is as good as positive rejection of the opportunity. James sums all of these distinctions and identifies a *genuine* option as one that is *live, forced,* and *momentous.* This conceptual background makes it possible to state the thesis of the "will to believe":

Our passional nature not only lawfully may, but must decide an option between propositions, whenever it is a genuine option that cannot by its nature be decided on intellectual grounds; for to say, under such circumstances, "Do not decide, but leave the question open," is itself a passional decision,—just like deciding yes or no— and is attended with the same risk of losing the truth.[4]

Before filling out the logic of the case, it should be understood that, as the wording of the thesis implies, James is making a particular case against a particular argument. He has narrowed the issue by making certain assumptions that exclude two kinds of positions— the absolutist and the skeptical—and establish his own empiricism as a starting point. As for the skeptic, "The postulate that there is truth and that it is the destiny of our minds to attain it, we are deliberately resolving to make, though the skeptic will not make it. We part company with him, therefore, absolutely, at this point."[5] Upon reviewing the endless and fruitless philosophical struggle to find a system of objective certitude, he concludes that "the trouble may all the time be essential, and that the intellect, even with truth directly in its grasp, may have no infallible signal for knowing whether it be true or no."[6] Thus, the issue is framed by the commitment to the search for truth precariously combined with a reticence and humility regarding the matter of certitude. The importance of the quest, along with the impossibility of a stable culmination, not only defines James's "radical" empiricism but stands as a rejection of those brands of "empiricism" that have effectively become absolutist. James explains:

But please observe, now, that when as empiricists we give up the doctrine of objective certitude, we do not thereby give up the quest or hope of truth itself. We still pin our faith on its existence, and still believe that we gain an ever better position towards it by systematically continuing to roll up experiences and think.[7]

The seemingly casual way in which the scope of the argument is trimmed down surely invites technical philosophical criticism, though the essay is not intended as a full expression of pragmatism. Such criticism might miss two points that are of greater relevance here. First, the very way in which the thesis is pruned is a case in point of the operation of the pragmatic method and spirit. James frames the issue as he does because that is the problem he is interested in, that is the point on which his doubts center, that is his "genuine option": the struggle between the passional and the intellectual in the resolution of judgments in the precarious search for truth. The issue is taken because of what Charles Peirce would call the irritating doubt that acts as the fillip to all inquiry.[8] This leads to the second point, that this genuine option is defined, at least in part, by the context in which he operates. In other words, James presents the whole matter within the setting of American currents of thought and the thesis deals with problems arising in that setting. There is, in James's technical statement of the problem, the same optimistic vitality, faith in the direction of experience, and rejection of *a priori* doctrine so characteristic of American thought. This feature of James's case, derived directly from his pragmatism, puts the consequences of his critique within the liberal tradition. Though these considerations jump ahead of the immediate issue, they should suggest why William James may be so helpful in shedding light on the dilemma at hand.

If the thrust of his case is not directed to the dead options of the skeptics and absolutists, what is James's option? Given the search for truth, and its tentativeness, he is concerned with those who dwell on the importance of the intellect being "coerced," as he has put it. Religiously they are agnostics, though that is probably not an adequate general term; in the secular realm they are a brand of empiricist. But before the full argument against this stance is presented, a further distinction must still be made. The distinction is between the desire to know the truth and the desire to avoid error, two very different motivations for the formation of beliefs, the choice between which "may end by coloring differently our whole intellectual life." Nervousness and fear of being duped conflict with the courage to take risks in the desire to get at the truth; the choice is that "we may regard the chase for truth as paramount, and the avoidance of error as secondary; or we may, on the other hand, treat the avoidance of error as more imperative, and let truth take its chance." James is clear about the kind of decision that has to be made between these two alternatives: "We must remember that these feelings of our duty about either truth or error are in any case only expressions of our passional life."9 In their strategy of inquiry, many would wish to wait until all the evidence is in, avoid the issues where their intellect cannot be coerced, and shun any error rather than take a chance on truth. In some situations, such as scientific investigation, this strategy may be quite justified, for in the facts of physical nature, "seldom is there any such hurry about them that the risks of being duped by believing a premature theory need be faced."10 James is quick to agree that dedication to reliable empirical evidence is commendable and, indeed, in the usual situation of science, a very worthy ideal for all to follow. But this only begs the critical question of the whole argument:

Are there not somewhere forced options in our speculative questions, and can we (as men who may be interested at least as much in positively gaining truth as in merely escaping dupery) always await with impunity till the coercive evidence shall have arrived?11

The various pieces of the argument begin to fit together in answer to this question.

The critical feature of a genuine option is the inability to be indifferent to it. Thus, a situation is defined in which a decision to avoid the issue is a decision about the issue—he who hesitates is lost. Those who would insist on the weight of sufficient evidence and ignore "passions" in forming beliefs would be very perplexed when confronted with a genuine option. The situation confounds their most admirable motives; in procrastinating over evidence, a vital and irreversible option may pass them by, their own "belief" is effectively established by default, and all of this occurs because of their desire to be cautious about error rather than courageous about truth—itself a position to which their intellects have not been coerced! The very notion of a genuine option means that the choice is over something important and consequential and the consequences of belief either will or will not come to pass; as James exemplifies it:

It is as if a man should hesitate indefinitely to ask a certain woman to marry him because he was not perfectly sure that she would prove an angel after he brought her home. Would he not cut himself off from that particular angel-possibility as decisively as if he went and married someone else?[12]

Though our intellect is not coerced in deciding on what basis to confront such a problem—avoid error or know truth—this is not to say that weighty justification cannot be presented one way or the other. But whichever way this justification goes, the point is already made that man's passional nature works its way into the whole process of formulating beliefs.

In reflecting on the original thesis, the reason "passion" enters our judgments is not because it represents an intrinsically superior means of arriving at the truth, but simply because life presents individuals with situations that cannot be dodged and that need to be confronted with whatever resources can be mustered. On the face of it, this conclusion is reached by making a judgment about the avoid-error/know-truth alternative, but there is another way to look at the issue. In at least one form, the commitment to avoid error is more than just a pusillanimous approach to truth-seeking. Rather, it includes an element of self-deception. This is the case when the investigator interprets his dalliance as an effective suspension of the issue, something that may be possible in the laboratory but perhaps not in real life. To avoid self-deception, he must admit that his hesitation may constitute a virtual rejection of an option but that he is willing to pay the price. Yet in the very act of escaping self-deception he runs against the original issue: Why should this price be paid? Is this the way to resolve issues of belief, by default of positive solution?

The two important premises of this argument—the contention

that there are genuine options and that the proper motivation is the desire to get at the truth—correspond respectively to what could be called the *pragmatic situation* and the *pragmatic spirit*. Within this situation and this spirit, man is not perfectly free to choose, *a priori*, any method he finds to his liking in forming his beliefs; rather, the will to believe, perhaps more correctly the *need* to believe, requires that man search out whatever available and effective resources he may have in dealing with life's toughest options. Indeed, the will to believe itself creates the opportunity to verify truth. The final verification may coerce our intellect, but can that point ever be reached if the first groping and hazardous steps are not taken? The real need to explore and test evokes a sense of venture, not timidity and diffidence, so that

it matters not to an empiricist from what quarter an hypothesis may come to him: he may have acquired it by fair means or by foul; passion may have whispered or accident suggested it; but if the total drift of thinking continue to confirm it, that is what he means by its being true.[13]

Clearly the *outcome* of inquiry, rather than strict methodology, is given preeminence according to this view; for what good is fastidious method, which is to assure us of truth, if it misses so much of its goal?

Consider this whole scheme of truth-seeking as it may apply to the study of man in political society. First, the world of political and social action can be unforgiving in the options it presents. As Ortega y Gasset once put it, "Politics is much more of a reality than science, because it is made up of unique situations in which a man suddenly finds himself submerged whether he will or no."[14] There is the hypothetical case of the voter who wants to vote intelligently and must decide between candidate A and candidate B, but wants to avoid any error in making his decision. He must have all the information needed to compel him to a choice and, without that data, judgment will be suspended. By introducing the ethic of the laboratory into the real world—suspend decision until your hypothesis can be proved (that A or B is closer to my views)—this imaginary citizen will have to brace himself for a long vigil. The world, however, does not wait upon such niceties. The time comes for a decision, the election is held, someone wins and fills the office, and all the while the commitment of this particular voter to a particular standard of proof has led him to abstain. Now there is nothing intrinsically illogical about a voter abstaining in an election, but in this case the abstention carried with it a particular significance—the attempt to avoid judgment where there was no solid ground of empirical proof. This is quite nonsensical to the extent that the voter is concerned with a genuine option in the real world; his abstention may be interpreted in many ways, but it surely was not completely without consequence. B wins, but would candidate A have been the great leader he was hypothesized to be? Who is to say? A voter's desire to keep the question open helped to cut off the possibility of ever knowing just as surely as if he had voted for his victorious opponent. The question could not remain literally open any more than the world could stop spinning.

A military commander facing a battle is in much the same demanding yet unwieldy situation. He may wish that his intelligence would confirm completely his capacity for victory, but, of course, he cannot wait with impunity for proof. A good leader may retreat, a good leader may press on with the battle, but a good leader is never caught by the enemy vacillating over his maps. Consider also the case of a jury deliberating the question of guilt or innocence. They may have the impulse to suspend judgment for lack of information and they may even find themselves without a verdict. But while the jury can hypothetically put itself in limbo, the defendant cannot; whatever they do, he is either behind bars or walking free. His condition reflects the consequence of a forced and momentous option, the pragmatic situation in which there is no alternative corresponding to a suspended decision of the jury. Finally, imagine a community confronted with a crisis such as an epidemic, a natural catastrophe, or perhaps an economic depression. They may confront the crisis effectively or ineffectively; they may suffer badly or survive well, but they are not afforded the luxury of committing themselves to complete inaction until a proven solution is found. There may be people who want to opt for such a course, but unless the demand for proof is satisfied quickly, this course will effectively permit the crisis to sustain itself. In sum, the positivist outlook may be of very little assistance to real world decision-makers.

The main concern at this point is not with the existence of such disjunctive options in public affairs but with justifiable guides for confronting such options—for the present their existence will be assumed. We may also assume, along with the pluralist, that the determination of what the public interest is is not subject to what

James would call "intellectual coercion." Two matters fall outside such positive coercion: matters of fact, mainly the prediction of the varied future consequences of an act, and value judgments. This distinction is ignored by James, for he is concerned with how one approaches the indeterminate element, whether it be factual or valuational; thus, he is concerned with how beliefs are formed and used as the basis for action regardless of whether they be beliefs about what *will* happen or about what *ought to* happen (though the former is more salient in his argument).

Thus, it has been assumed that the public affairs of a society encompass disjunctive and indeterminate alternatives, that is, live and uncoerced options. The indeterminate character of such options is paramount to all of those critics of the public interest who have raised the questions, "Who is to say and how is one to say what the public interest is?" The issue concerns how such a question should be dealt with. One attempted resolution would suggest that since the matter is indeterminate, since no one has been able to prove that particular alternatives represent the public interest, since no one has even been able to say satisfactorily what the public interest is theoretically, the whole concept is meaningless and may be dismissed from technical language, and the issues accompanying it are false issues. It is not intellectually meaningful or realistic to ask what goals or directions a society should pursue.

The charge of "meaninglessness" included in this resolution of the matter leads directly into the pragmatist's concern with consequences of action. For James, the option's meaningfulness is established by the disjunctive character of the possible consequences and by the genuineness of the option, not by whether the option is subject to rigorous standards of proof. James would argue that the charge of meaninglessness is a case of "vicious intellectualism," in which the meaning of a problem is established by an *a priori* commitment to method rather than by the existential context of the problem. Schubert did not see that the concept could be operationalized within the framework of social science methodology as he perceived it, and the concept thus lacked meaning and significance for him. James's charge is that such a view is hopelessly intellectualist, abstract, and divorced from concrete reality. The option of operating with or operating without some view of the public interest has meaning to the extent that there are important, significant consequences one way or the other. If the public interest includes disjunctive options that a society must confront, then these options represent a meaningful human situation.

The question of meaning is to some extent a corollary to the assumption that the public affairs of a society may present genuine options; at this juncture, the more important issue is how to confront the indeterminateness of such options. The "meaninglessness" charge suggests a strict skeptical approach that would view indeterminateness as intellectually untouchable. But since the indeterminate subject happens to be a genuine option, the issue substantially changes. The issue is not whether the option can be ignored with impunity but whether it is worth paying the price to be, as James puts it, on the side of avoiding error rather than searching out the truth. The option is real and meaningful, but the choices to be made are not subject to "intellectual coercion." What is to be done? Take the safe road, speak and judge only with absolute assurance and suffer the consequences that will come by default of action, or take the precarious route, walking on eggshells to find the best way you can. James's preference, on the one hand, is visceral; confronted with such a situation, his taste is for risk-taking. He explains that "Whenever there is no forced option, the dispassionately judicial intellect with no pet hypothesis, saving us, as it does, from dupery at any rate, ought to be our ideal."[15] In the case of a forced option there is no such luxury as waiting for all the evidence to come in:

It seems *a priori* improbable that the truth should be so nicely adjusted to our needs and powers as that. In the great boarding-house of nature, the cakes and the butter and the syrup seldom come out so even and leave the plate so clean. Indeed, we should view them with scientific suspicion if they did.[16]

However, the "pragmatic spirit" behind James's preference is not the critical element in the argument. What is critical is that the avoid-error/search-truth alternative is itself a "passional decision." How is the skeptic going to justify taking the safe road when faced with a forced option? How can the justification satisfy his positivist commitments? What proof is there for resolving a consequential issue by taking the safe road? The public interest is an indeterminate thing, but it is equally indeterminate (i.e., not subject to being "coerced" by the facts) what type of assumption should be used in forming our belief about it. If the whole theoretical and practical issue of the public interest is consequential, some pressing evidence suggests that it is more sensible to "search out the truth" in it, the main evidence being the default of control over consequences that results if the issue is ignored for want of positive knowledge and information. But the main point is still that having reached the avoid-error/search-truth choice, the issue has been taken out of the skeptic's bailiwick. The question is not how to prove that there is a public interest; the question is to confront or not confront the stubborn, unavoidable, and indeterminate dilemmas raised by the idea of the public interest.

James's challenge to the kind of thinking behind the attack on the public interest can best be summarized in his own words:

This at least is certain,—that the world of our present natural knowledge *is* enveloped in a larger world of *some* sort of whose residual properties we at present can frame no positive idea.

Agnostic positivism, of course, admits this principle theoretically in the most cordial terms, but insists that we must not turn it to any practical use. We have no right, this doctrine tells us, to dream dreams, or suppose anything about the unseen part of the universe, merely because to do so may be for what we are pleased to call our highest interests. We must always wait for sensible evidence for our beliefs; and where such evidence is inaccessible we must frame no hypotheses whatever. Of course, this is a safe enough position *in abstracto.* If a thinker had no stake in the unknown, no vital needs, to live or languish according to what the unseen world contained, a philosophic neutrality and refusal to believe either one way or the other would be his wisest cue. But, unfortunately, neutrality is not only inwardly difficult, it is also outwardly unrealizable, where our relations to an alternative are practical and vital. . . . There are, you see, inevitable occasions in life when *inaction is a kind of action,* and when not to be for is to be practically against; and in all such cases strict and consistent neutrality is an unattainable thing.[17]

The point of this argument is that the significance of the public interest concept can be established independent of the existing consciousness of political actors and of positive, operational criteria. The significance that is established results from an analysis of the objective consequences of decisions and non-decisions. The political actor may not appreciate the character of genuine options as described by James, but does that mean he is immune to the consequences of such options? As for political science, that the public interest refers to indeterminate genuine options is hardly a sufficient basis on which to reject the concept. The weight of the argument, of course, depends on the assumption, yet to be taken up, that the public interest can be said to identify those situations that James calls genuine options.

Before we move on, an earlier observation requires further attention. It was noted that the indeterminate element in human judgments, those elements about which evidence and proof are incomplete, could be of two kinds—facts or values—and it was further noted that the distinction did not seem important to James in making his case. In rebuttal to James it might be argued that the distinction is important in that facts and values, though both indeterminate, may be indeterminate in different ways. Facts may be indeterminate for merely circumstantial reasons—a conceptualization of facts may be easily operationalized and theoretically testable, though the actual methods to be employed may need refinement, may be too expensive for convenient use, or the existing strategies of inquiry may simply be too massive to muster easily. The problem of interviewing every registered voter in the United States about his voting habits is mainly a logistical problem and does not, of itself, raise conceptual problems beyond the voting studies already done. The indeterminate element involved in not interviewing every voter is only a result of relating a statistical universe to a statistical sample, with acceptable levels of probability, so as to make the research task manageable. With valuational issues it is a different matter, since the skeptic/positivist critic claims that the indeterminate character of values cannot even be hypothetically resolved through the use of better methods; values present a qualitatively different problem. The critic argues that we do not even know how to go about positing values in such a way that they will "coerce our intellect" in the same way that brute facts will impinge themselves on us.

James's counter to this is central to his pragmatic view of the world. Essentially, his argument is that certain facts cannot be tested without the intervening commitment to a value that stirs one to take an action that provides the only possible context for the test. James's example of this, cited above, is the case of the man trying to determine whether or not he would be happy being married to a particular woman. The longer he hesitates over the issue while waiting for all of the evidence to be in, the longer he cuts himself off from real decisive knowledge of his possible happiness. If he waits long enough he may never really know the answer at all. If he enters the marriage he may not only posit the truth he was looking for, he may indeed create the truth by the vigor with which he carries out the commitment to the relationship. Knowing the truth and actually "having all the evidence in" may be dependent upon human action based on value judgments. There are many involved issues here concerning the relation between human thought and action, issues that may be clarified later on in trying to find out what the public interest really means, but the important point for the moment is that the indeterminate character of facts and values may be interdependent and that there is no qualitative difference between the two that is critical to James's case.

In sum, James offers an alternative view of how a particular idea can be considered meaningful, a view derived from an analysis of the context of forming beliefs and making judgments in consequential human situations and not derived from an abstract, *a priori* commitment to methods of proof. In James's sense, the public interest could be meaningful even though it encompasses many indeterminate elements. The purpose of introducing James's argument is to show that the public interest may be a case in point of the general considerations relating to human beliefs, values, and judgments. James establishes the approach that must be taken in deciding how the concept of the public interest will be treated. Does it identify genuine options that men must face? If so, inability to "prove" that the particular interest of the public is such-and-such does not mitigate the meaningfulness or the import of the concept and the attendant problems it raises. Thus, the groundwork is laid for showing how the public interest can be a legitimate theoretical and practical consideration, even though it appears to resist all attempts to give it purely positive, empirical significance. The "passional" side of man comes into play in seeking out the truth because of the conditions under which man seeks truth and forms beliefs about it. Among those conditions are the compelling choices men must make about their collective quality of life and it is necessary to show that these choices constitute genuine options.

NOTES

1. William James, *The Will to Believe*, pp. 1–2.
2. James, pp. 2–3.
3. The following set of concepts is summarized from James, pp. 2–4.
4. James, p. 11.
5. James, p. 12.
6. James, p. 16.
7. James, p. 17; see also James, pp. 13–14.
8. Charles S. Peirce, *Philosophical Writings of Peirce*, pp. 9–11.
9. This series of quotes is from James, p. 18.
10. James, p. 20.
11. James, p. 22.
12. James, p. 26.
13. James, p. 17.
14. Ortega y Gasset, p. 158.
15. James, pp. 21–22.
16. James, p. 22.
17. James, pp. 54–55.

CHAPTER THREE

DEWEY: EMPIRICAL CONSIDERATIONS REGARDING THE PUBLIC

The assumption of the previous chapter—that the public interest does identify what may be called "genuine options"—must now be examined more closely. This requires an empirical referent for the idea of a *public* set of options.

At this juncture some comment must be made about the phrase "public interest" and its component terms. The phrase is theoretically ambiguous and can be used in different ways. It may refer to certain values or goals that are, as is often said, "*in* the public interest"; in this sense it presumes to suggest what the public wants or needs. But it also may be used to identify, in merely descriptive fashion, that a given topic or set of affairs is a matter of public rather than private concern. In fact, these two uses have their parallels in the way the term "private interest" is used—that is, it may identify a person's wants, desires or needs (it is in my interest to live in this neighborhood), or it may merely identify those affairs that are relevant to him and within his competence to affect (the whole matter of where I live is of personal interest to me). Though it may be tempting to refer to these kinds of meanings as "normative" and "descriptive," it may be more correct and more useful to refer to them as the particular and the general references of the public interest, the former referring to the identification of explicit goals and purposes and the latter to a collection of alternative goals and strategies that define a context of decision and action. In examining the character of the hypothetical options that have been raised, it is necessary not only to see whether they are "genuine" but also to establish that there is a "public" to which the options are relevant and that there is some way of establishing what "interest" means. Clarifying the empirical meaning of those component terms should provide the analytical setting for identifying the kind of problems raised in relation to the public interest; more specifically, it should help in understanding the particular and general uses of the concept.

As for the term "public," it refers here to a group of people, e.g., all the citizens of a state; or, as an adjective, it may be used to characterize something as relevant to the whole people, e.g., the "public sector" of the economy. The question is how to pin down these two related uses of the term to their concrete empirical significance. Even those who may deny that the public can have an interest may not necessarily abandon the use of the term "public," for example, in reference to "public policy-making." This use, however, may only be meant to indicate those affairs falling in the bailiwick of government as opposed to private organizations and institutions; thus, the difference between the public and private sectors is only derivative of the difference between two sets of social institutions, which only begs the question.

John Dewey has offered perhaps the most constructive empirical observations about the use of the term "public." Briefly, Dewey contends that the root fact is that human actions have consequences on others, and that from this the distinction can be made between direct consequences upon those immediately a party to a social transaction and indirect consequences upon others. Upon this distinction between direct and indirect consequences of human action Dewey rests the distinction between private and public, the latter identifying those who are affected by the indirect consequences of private acts.[1] This view of Dewey's public is accepted by some pluralists—even though they have no use for the notion of a public interest—and they find it consistent with group theory. David Truman adopts Dewey's meaning of "public" and uses it as the basis for analyzing politics in terms of "many publics." Thus, "an interest group is a segment of a public that shares a similar view of, or attitude toward, the consequences under discussion."[2] There is a plurality of interest groups on the one hand and on the other, and at a higher level, there is a plurality of publics, their diversity resulting from the various issue areas, i.e., kinds of indirect consequences. For Truman, Dewey's conceptualization of the public is helpful and certainly does not disrupt his group theory of politics. Bernard Hennessy, in his book on public opinion, also suggests a pluralist gloss of Dewey, to whom he attributes the view that

there are many publics . . . such that each issue creates its own public, and these publics will normally not consist of the same individuals who make up any other particular publics, although every individual will, at any given time, be a member of many other publics.[3]

Within any of these publics, there forms a "complex of beliefs," which is to say that "the interested public will divide itself into two or more points of view."[4] For both Truman and Hennessy, a public then only identifies a cluster of interests, and society consists of several publics that represent simply another tier of pluralism.[5]

The above interpretations are a serious misrepresentation of Dewey's position. A closer look makes it clear that Dewey dwelt on the indirect consequences of social transactions for the purpose of identifying The Public and relating it to the basis of state organization. The direct consequences of a social transaction are regulated by the participants; similarly, "when indirect consequences are recognized and there is effort to regulate them, something having the traits of a state comes into existence."[6] Since the public identifies the objects of that association known as the state, a connection develops between things that are "public" and things "official," contrary to "private" things; in Dewey's own words:

The public consists of all those who are affected by the indirect consequences of transactions to such an extent that it is deemed necessary to have those consequences systematically cared for. Officials are those who look out for and take care of the interests thus affected. Since those who are indirectly affected are not direct participants in the transactions in question, it is necessary that certain persons be set apart to represent them, and see to it that their interests are conserved and protected. . . . The public as far as organized by means of officials and material agencies to care for the extensive and enduring indirect consequences of transactions between persons is the Populus.[7]

Clearly, the public is meant here to identify, not a plural collection of issue areas, but the very connecting link that joins people together in a state; the state manifests itself as a human response to the need to regulate indirect consequences. Further elaborating, Dewey explains:

Consequences have to be taken care of, looked out for. This supervision and regulation cannot be effected by the primary groupings themselves. . . . The obvious external mark of the organization of a public or of a state is thus the existence of officials.[8]

Dewey often alludes to the "general" use of the public interest, mentioned above, as in the statement that "the state is the organization of the public effected through officials for the protection of the interests shared by its members." "Interests" refers to the consequences that define a shared context of decision and action. This view of the public as the basis of the state is meant to be an empirically based, non-static conception of the state as a human association; hence Dewey emphasizes that

conditions make the consequences of associated action and the knowledge of them different[9] . . . the formation of states must be an experimental process . . . the State must always be rediscovered. . . . It is not the business of political philosophy and science to determine what the state in general should or must be.[10]

Dewey clearly uses his empirical conception of the public to get at the meaning of the state and its all-inclusive character, rather than merely to identify another tier of pluralism.[11] Given the plural character of interests in society, it is necessary to discover what holds society together in the first place; Dewey's answer is "the public," which is formed from the consequences of human action that call for regulation. The public is thus all-inclusive in membership, being in a sense coterminous with the membership of the state, though those affairs that may be designated "public" may be, at any particular time, very limited. Thus, the state is, at one and the same time, both a real social whole and a limited human enterprise, limited and defined by the need to regulate indirect consequences of human action.

True, Dewey admits that there are different points of view about how to cope with public issues, but the pluralists have still misinterpreted this point. For Dewey, these differences of viewpoint are over the question of how to regulate and control the indirect consequences of social transactions; any particular viewpoint or "interest" is an expression of concern about how public consequences will be arranged, that is, about what the condition of public life will be like. On the contrary, the "interests" Truman and Hennessy conceive of are built around the oversight of the direct consequences of primary social transactions; such oversight obviously will have an effect on indirect consequences—indeed, it will generate them—but such interests are not specifically addressed to the "social interest." Thus, what could be called a faction within the public is not identifiable merely by its attempts to use the processes of politics and government, but rather by its attempts to use such processes for particular purposes, i.e., the promotion of a particular point of view regarding the disposition of those affairs that constitute the social interest.[12] For example, an industrialist may be very concerned about legislation designed to control pollution because of how it may relate to his company's growth and profits. He may exert himself to influence the legislation to his advantage, he may be very effective in doing so, and his actions may result in diffuse consequences for the physical environment. But all of this behavior is quite different from the actions of a person concerned with the indirect ecological consequences of pollution as such; the industrialist may act without the slightest consciousness of such consequences or without such consciousness in any way influencing his actions. This distinction between direct and indirect consequences is the basis for seeing "public" and "private" as fundamentally different orientations. Thus, there can be different kinds of factions in society depending on which kinds of consequences the division is about. In this way, "official" behavior is distinguished from "private" behavior, with the former including the behavior of people in their role as citizens contrary to their role as protector of private stakes. To correct any misrepresentation, it must be understood that when Dewey refers to the public he is speaking of something more than a specific issue area, and in referring to the intricate processes that go into forming public action he is speaking of something distinct from the interplay of private interests. Only with such clarification is it possible to appreciate that Dewey is not being merely histrionic in talking of

the conditions which must be fulfilled if the Great Society is to become a Great Community; a society in which the ever-expanding and intricately ramifying consequences of associated activities shall be known in the full sense of that word, so that an organized, articulate Public comes into being.[13]

Before using Dewey's conception of the public, it is necessary to comment upon the term "interest." It was noted that the term has both a particular and a general application. In its general application, the public interest refers to the affairs of the public—the indirect consequences; and, in this sense, identifying those interests that happen to be public is a fairly objective, empirical matter subject to many conventional modes of analysis. This meaning of interest, when linked to the term "public," is closely tied to what Dewey means by the public itself. If one establishes that the conjoint behavior of A and B is generating indirect consequences affecting many others beyond A and B, then those "others" have an interest in—or at least a potential interest in—those consequences. Thus, the general meaning of public interest refers to a concrete set of consequences that present a possible object of attention to the public, those affected by the consequences. And when someone talks about the public interest, the possibility exists of identifying whether or not the realm of issues has been properly identified by the speaker as "public."

Aside from the objective and concrete significance of the term "interest," it also, and perhaps more frequently, designates the conscious orientation of an individual or group. The articulation, identification, perception, and evaluation of an interest is a major variable. The objective character of interests must be understood and appreciated, and the response to the interest must be determined, and all of this can be done with varying degrees of success or not at all. In the case of the general use of the term "interest," there is the problem of being properly aware of what aspects of reality are leading to what kinds of consequences, of what they are and of how important they are and, indeed, of whether or not they are actually public in character. In this way it is possible to talk of the varying level of awareness of public consequences that represents a particular society's conception of the public interest as the affairs of the public. This discussion of the general way of applying the term public interest discloses two apparent references: 1) to the indirect consequences themselves as the public's business or affairs and, 2) to the consciousness or awareness that any specific public has of any common affairs. Obviously the empirical scope of the two references can and most likely will be different. These two references may be similar to the distinction between wants and needs, a distinction that will become important in later discussion. The important point at this stage in the argument is that although indirect consequences may go unattended, they still stand as a usable measure to be invoked when a claim is made that something is a matter of *public* interest.

Interest means not only an area of concern designated by concrete reality and/or human awareness and attentiveness, it also indicates particular goals, values, opinions, and points of view in relation to the general area of concern. Frequently, the particular over the general use of the term is at work when the question is asked what the public interest is. At this juncture the classic problems of the public interest arise. The actual carrying out of an action in the name of the public interest involves determinations of value; values are seen as relative and non-provable, yet the state agencies—which are concrete manifestations of Dewey's public— involve the use of coercive force. The problems with this situation cannot be completely resolved by appeal to an analogy between public and private interests because unlike the former, the latter may be the subject of voluntary action and individual self-determination. A private group does not have to monopolize force to protect and promote its interest, but does not the public have to coerce in order to pursue its interest? Is it not perhaps better then to deny the state the role of articulating a public interest?

Before jumping to a discussion of these problems of the particular public interest, the empirical basis of these issues must be understood. Several basic facts are susceptible to observation and testing both by the political scientist and the political actor: 1) the existence of a public, 2) an interest that identifies the affairs of the public, and 3) the genuineness of the options that the public confronts in its attempt to control and regulate its affairs. The first two items can be treated together since Dewey's conception of the public includes the notion that the public has an interest, at least in a general and objective sense, which is to say that there are concrete and observable consequences that establish the boundaries of the public's affairs. If the rejoinder of the group theorist is that the disposition of these affairs can still be explained by reference to the workings of private interests, he is correct, but only partially correct. The group theorist is only telling how a particular society has decided to deal with its public affairs; nothing in his case explains how these affairs are thereby less public. The observation that there is very little consciousness of indirect consequences of behavior may be true, and probably is true in America, but that does not necessarily affect the existence and the ramifications of such indirect consequences. Thus, the political analyst may be able to develop a viable conception of the public interest even where there is little political consciousness of it. The pivotal factor is the ability to make a meaningful empirical distinction between direct and indirect consequences of social transactions. What is needed in the study of public policy are effective measures of the scope of consequences and criteria for identifying the point where consequences spill out beyond the realm of private activity.

A further point regarding the testing of these concepts is that there is no need to show that the indirect consequences touch absolutely everyone at one particular time. In specific instances the consequences may only be potential; also, one type of indirect consequence is the limitation on human choice resulting from the need to escape the threat of certain actual consequences. Thus, the fact that one lives in the only location in America thoroughly free of air pollution (reportedly Flagstaff, Arizona) does not isolate him from the public problem of air pollution. Ecological destruction need not be total before it is understood to be a matter of the public interest. Similarly, civil rights problems may seem to be susceptible to group analysis, and since the affected group may seem to be a clearly defined minority, the indirect consequences for the public may not be apparent. The decade of the 1960s should have been sufficient to disabuse people of such analysis. Of course, one of the difficulties of realizing the comprehensiveness of indirect consequences is the very fact that they are indirect; their identification may require some analytical reflection. The white suburbanite may feel that the "race problem" is of no consequence to him, which is quite ironic if he became a suburbanite in order to escape the problem. The very act of escape manifests the real and diffuse consequences set in motion which, for this person, may have determined where he would live, the kind of house he would own, the range of price he would have to pay, the need to commute to work and the need to purchase another car for his family. This may be said to be an example of individual expression of private economic self-interest, but it may be viewed as a particular person's way of reacting to a complex set of indirect consequences of the race relations prevalent in the society. If viewed in the second way, would it still be meaningful to analyze the situation in terms of an urban interest and a suburban interest? From Dewey's perspective, this suburbanite might be said to be engaging in a private, individual response to a set of conditions that are objectively public in character. Viewed in this way, a number of fascinating issues arise that are hidden by the "private interest" interpretation. Is the individual response to public problems satisfying to the individual? What are the effects on the seriousness of the public problem? Is it lessened? Or does this situation breed a sense of frustration and powerlessness? Is there a mistaken sense of individual efficacy here that is the cause of embitterment toward political institutions in a free and open society? Has the incessant need to slice up the most momentous social issues into tidy interests, the unvaried commitment to variety and plurality, and the assumption of the willfulness and effectiveness of private self-interest kept political analysis from understanding the source of a number of critical political problems?

At this point, it may be appropriate to note that Dewey's conception of the public tends to generate two quite opposite critical reactions. For some, the notion of direct and indirect consequences would seem to assert the primacy of private interests and a limited or incidental function for the state, giving this view a distinctly liberal flavor. Yet it may also be argued that the pragmatic way of determining the range of the public and the ubiquity of indirect consequences makes Dewey's public potentially statist and totalitarian. The confusion can be cleared up by noting that the concept "public" does not necessarily, by definition, justify either interpretation. The point of the argument is that the range of the public is itself a matter of political determination, that it has no natural or fixed boundaries that can be rationally set down. Part of the confusion is the prevalent liberal attitude that private concerns, free of governmental interference, have somehow been removed *a priori* from the realm of public affairs. This is quite mistaken; the very opposite seems to be the case. Rights of private property, for example, rather than being an indication that property ownership is an affair outside the public realm, constitute a statement of how the body politic is prepared to confront the matter of ownership and its consequences. This merely points up the fact that in controlling and regulating indirect consequences, one suitable strategy is *laissez-faire;* thus, in the final analysis, private rights are political, not natural, creations.

Finally, the third item mentioned above may be directly examined: Does the idea of the public interest identify genuine options that a society confronts? As was seen, based on Dewey's view of the public, the public interest may refer to a concrete set of options, a set of alternative responses to the indirect consequences of social transactions combined with the consciousness of this set of options. It should be recalled that the very criteria of the genuineness of an option consisted of a mixture of such objective and subjective elements. How do these indirect consequences and the set of optional responses to the need to control them size up against the criteria of a "genuine option"? The question of whether they are *living* options depends on whether the component hypotheses represent real possibilities, both materially and consciously (i.e., it "makes some appeal to your belief"). For contemporary Americans the choice between their present society and the recreation of a life similar to ancient Athens is a dead option: it neither is materially within reason, nor does it appeal, in even a small way, to their beliefs. Other choices, however, are *live* and public, such as the choice between free enterprise and economic regulation. The various conceivable forms that the indirect consequences *might* take represent the *liveness* of the opinions concerning them.

More importantly, the choice must be *forced;* it must be understood to be a logical disjunction where there is no possibility of avoidance. For the public it may be the choice between preserving the natural resources of the society or having them degenerate; or, more generally, it may be the choice between a rich or a poor society, a free or an oppressive society. Using the example of natural resources, it can be shown how a disjunctive option forms for a society: private actions of individuals and groups affect various resources; because of the character of the ecological system, there are numerous diffuse and indirect consequences to the way resources are treated privately; the public then confronts the alternative of conserving resources or of not doing so and any attempt to default on the issue, to avoid it entirely, is the equivalent of having decided against the preservation of resources—the option is forced.

James finally suggested that a genuine option must be *momentous,* an irreversible and unique opportunity with significant stakes, and though such a criterion may seem rather inexact, it should be clear that the public must necessarily encounter the most momentous of options. All of the examples of live and forced options already given are surely momentous for a society. Though

Dewey realized that the scope of the public may be very limited, nevertheless controlling the indirect consequences of action is a task with widespread and critical ramifications for the quality of life in a society. History itself marks the momentous options that various societies have faced, options that give each society its distinctive traits.

Having laid the groundwork with Dewey's empirical view of the "public," and using "interest" to designate, in its general sense, an area of concern in relation to which there may be many optional responses, it has been possible to show what is meant by saying that the public interest involves genuine options for a society. The component hypotheses that make up an option refer to corresponding views of the public interest taken in its particular usage. This constitutes the critical assumption behind the argument in the previous chapter, an assumption that is fully subject to observation and analysis for the purpose of filling out in detail the status of the public interest in a particular society at a particular time. But there is one further issue—the very acceptance or rejection of the idea of a public interest is itself a genuine option. Will the indirect consequences be recognized for what they are? Will there be an attentiveness to them and a willingness to confront them? Will they be ignored and thus determined and regulated by default? These issues simply manifest the second assumption made by James: that there is a necessary choice to be made between the inclination to search for truth versus the inclination to avoid error, a choice that is indeterminate. The society's consciousness of the public interest, whether it even sees that there are such matters to be considered, may be itself a fundamental public option.

At this point it should be easier to appreciate that the public interest does not involve any special mystery or enigma, nor is it a mere bit of philosophical patois, nor a turgid prop of political rhetoric. The term identifies perfectly concrete issues and problems that face any society and it identifies the kinds of responses to these problems that society generates. The public interest—in the sense of the "affairs of the public," at least—is as real as the social system and political system themselves; it is conceptually related to the very basis of associational life—men coming together to share a task. There is no doubt that a full inquiry into the significance of the public interest raises fundamental and formidable dilemmas and these dilemmas ultimately relate to the very nature of politics itself.

NOTES

1. John Dewey, *The Public and its Problems,* pp. 12–17.
2. David Truman, p. 218.
3. Bernard Hennessy, p. 99.
4. Hennessy, p. 100.
5. In relation to the problem of "The Public" versus "many publics," D. G. Smith has tried to establish a close relationship between pragmatism and the group theory of politics, yet he presumes such an intimate connection that his discussion results in a massive analytical imbroglio in which Dewey is criticized for being ambiguous and incomplete. See Smith, pp. 600–610. It would have been much less painful, not to mention more accurate, had Smith simply admitted that the two schools are not the same, that there are differences that are not mere ambiguities, and that this in no way denies that they are "closely related both historically and philosophically." Because these admissions are made, a much better treatment of the relationship is offered by John P. East, pp. 597–605.
6. Dewey, p. 12.
7. Dewey, pp. 15–16.
8. Dewey, p. 27.
9. Dewey, p. 33.
10. Dewey, pp. 33–34.
11. "Our doctrine of plural forms is a statement of fact: that there exist a plurality of social groupings, good, bad and indifferent. . . . It does not intimate that the function of the state is limited to settling conflicts among other groups, as if each one of them had a fixed scope of action of its own. Were that true, the state would be only an umpire. . . ." Dewey, p. 73.
12. Typical conceptualizations have identified the "political" character of interest groups by reference to their method of action and without consideration to the scope of their purpose; for example: "When an organized group decides to bring its case to the government, it is a pressure group or political interest group." Hugh Bone and Austin Ranney, p. 64.
13. Dewey, p. 184.

CHAPTER FOUR

THE PROBLEM
OF THE PUBLIC INTEREST

To this point the purpose of the discussion has been quite limited —to show that the public interest refers to aspects of political life that are significant, consequential, and concrete. The concept of the public interest and the problems it raises cannot be dismissed out of hand, ignored, or avoided if there is a desire for a full understanding of the behavior of men organized in a state. The fundamental notion of the public interest is empirically rooted in the nature of the political organization of a state. The empirical assumption is that society *qua* society includes shared affairs of life that derive from immediate human association in the form of the indirect consequences of such association. The common condition is different from, say, the physical environment and it gives shape to the public, those sharing this common condition.

Insofar as men politically organize in a society to perform tasks relevant to their common condition, the purposes they articulate and the actions they take can be analyzed in terms of options that they confront; the different alternatives making up an option may be thought of as hypotheses. So far, one use of the "public interest" has been to designate the common condition and the society's awareness of it; in this general sense the public interest simply means that which is of interest to the public or that which is a public area of concern. The fact that a particular society at a particular time appears to have, on the basis of empirical evidence, no articulate consciousness of the public interest does not disturb the empirical character of the concept.

The common condition not only marks off the characteristic tasks of the state but also generates options that will at times be "genuine options" as described by William James. Thus, the possible responses to the common condition are usually (though not necessarily in every case) of a particular character: they are live, momentous, forced, and disjunctive options. In a concrete sense, the options cannot be avoided; they are such that to ignore them is, in effect, to have them decided by default, to have the outcome imposed by circumstances rather than conscious action. If the possibility of avoidance is self-deceptive and unattractive (and the default of human power and control will necessarily be an unattractive prospect for many people), the prospect of socially confronting the option head on is also problematic. It is problematic because it leads directly into the issues of human thought and action, of determining collective goals and purposes while preserving the integrity of the individual. It throws one directly into the imbroglio of dichotomies that haunt man's political life: reality versus ideals; society versus the individual; freedom versus . authority; public versus private. For many, the weight of these issues has led them to attack their very origin—the "myth" and "ghost" of the public interest. But the sheer weight and scope of these problems should not mistakenly lead one into easy answers, the easiest of all being the contention that, as they are related to the public interest, they are not even real or meaningful. The pragmatist appreciates, in the authentic spirit of empiricism, that meaningful issues of human inquiry and action are not identified by their susceptibility to positive and "coercive" methods of proof, but by their consequential importance to human life. The acceptance or avoidance of the dilemmas at hand makes a real difference as to whether or not the common conditions of life may be made, as much as is possible, subject to conscious human control and regulation; thus, they have a concrete and material meaning. The unwieldy and indeterminate character of these issues in no way mitigates their meaning and significance for political man.

The most serious problems relate to the *particular* use of the public interest concept. Once the general use of the term is established, i.e., to indicate those things that are of interest to the public, its particular application is derivative, i.e., the public interest designates the alternatives that are, or may be, chosen and pursued in the attempt to regulate consequences. The particular is what is most often in mind when the question is asked what the public interest is. This is the indeterminate issue that is not necessarily subject to the "coercion of our intellect" but that has to be decided because it derives from the general public interest seen as a set of genuine options. At this point it is possible to offer a cogent, though partial, answer to the question of what the public interest means. In *general* terms, it means the indirect consequences of social transactions seen as the affairs of the people organized in the association known as the state. In *particular* terms, it means the goals and strategies society may articulate and pursue for the purpose of regulating and controlling the common condition. The particular public interest may be more conveniently referred to as the *public good*.

If this is what the public interest means in its broad conceptual form, then the so-called "problems of the public interest" that have been referred to are problems of filling out the meaning in specific contexts. In other words, how does the public good come to be determined? This is clearly a problem of political action, though perhaps less obviously it is also a problem of formal political inquiry; such inquiry, to be truly relevant, to take its lead from concrete problems of human behavior, must muster whatever resources it can to clarify and make more reasonable the process of judging what the public interest is. To say that this process is indeterminate is not to say that it does not benefit at all from formal investigation; if political science is to offer something of real social value, then one of its objectives should be to shed light wherever it can and as well as it can on such vital questions. Insofar as the public interest is a problem of political action, it is one thing to say that one is willing to pay the costs of neglecting it (he would rather be sure of avoiding error than precariously searching out the truth), and quite another thing to say that the problem is meaningless. The above argument is intended to show that the latter position is untenable, and as for the former, the purpose of investigating the problems is to make clear what alternatives there are to letting the common condition take shape through default of any attempt at collective human control.

A need exists to clarify exactly why a determination of the particular public interest is so problematic. The issues that it encompasses are surely not unique to the investigations of social and behavioral sciences. Even aside from the workings of the public, one finds people forming groups, sharing values and goals, taking joint action, trying to decide their fate, behaving gregariously, and these are all accepted as phenomena subject to accepted techniques of analysis. If all of these matters are so common, then why do they become so perplexing when used in reference to the public? The answer is that problems arise because of the difference between private interest groups and the public as a group. Since both are types of human groups built around purposeful action, there will be some similarities in group behavior and dynamics; yet a critical difference results from the all-inclusive character of the public. The formation of private interest group action is easily reducible to individual initiatives, orientations, and life situations because the scope of the members' orientations and the scope of the organization's goals are coterminous almost by definition. One joins a group to protect and promote certain particular goals already fairly well identified by both the group and the individual. The group is like a partial extension of the individual: a situation that is maximally achieved where there is individual freedom of judgment and action.

With the public it is quite a different matter. Except in certain figurative and legalistic ways, one does not join the public in the way that one joins a secondary social group. Indeed, if Dewey is to be taken as a guide, the very formation of the public is based on things that happen to people almost inadvertently. Two strangers are engaging in activities that have repercussions for you and many other people, and those who are affected come together to do something to manage the consequences. Despite the primitiveness of this characterization, it does highlight the unique aspect of the public—that is, the public forms, not out of the need to do a particular thing, but out of the need to do something! Unlike private interest, the public does not determine as a part of the principle of its formation what its actual goals and values are but only that there is a shared fate that requires some action. The interest group in some way specifies at the outset what its goals are; the public, at a minimum, is only aware of the need to deal with the common condition—but in what way and to what end? The root causes of its formation precede any particular answer to such questions. Each individual is put in the awkward position of being in the same boat with everyone else, yet not being sure who is the captain and where they are going. One way or another they will find some direction, but it is not given to them by virtue of being in the public group.

When reference is made to the problem of determining the public good, the difficulty goes beyond the fact that valuational issues are at stake; rather, the problem of the public good is a result of the peculiar condition of the public. What is curious about the formation of the public, as Dewey has described it, is that it derives its identity from objective shared conditions (indirect consequences) while at the same time there is a lack of any original, congenital direction or goal for the public. The fact of the public's existence leaves unanswered the issue of its purpose. In contrast, in other realms of life, certain directing values may be "given" or set by necessity; in Aristotle's terms it is the distinction between "mere life" and the "good life," the latter being an area for human deliberation.[1] The essence of the public's dilemma can be summed up in the idea that its very existence is characterized by a mixture of necessity and uncertainty or, perhaps more accurately, the necessity of uncertainty. Necessity here takes the form of a "need to act" as defined by James's conception of genuine options, the irretrievable, unavoidable life decisions; uncertainty and indeterminateness are contained in the fact that the necessary questions of public choice have no necessary answers.

The necessity of the political association has not been as deeply appreciated since the introduction of the liberal conception of voluntarism as the basis of the citizen's identity, and the sociological treatment of the state as an association or secondary group in the same analytical category as social groups generally and distinguished by such things as its monopoly of force. Though not necessarily inaccurate, as far as they go, these conceptions give a certain plausibility to the modern issue of an "escape from politics" and the image of man against government. The Paine-Madison-Calhoun distinction between society and government and the view of government as a "necessary evil" is, ironically, more the result of liberal voluntarism than of any precise conception of the necessity of political association. The concept of a voluntary consent to a social contract need not be considered thoroughly inconsistent with the necessity of which we are speaking here. The issues of establishing authority and generating responses to public problems may certainly benefit from the contract metaphor, but this should not be expanded to suggest that there is some choice for or against politics—that is, that there can be a choice against politics that is anything other than a tragic resignation from the reality of the human condition or else a grand delusion. Isaiah Berlin, in commenting upon the realization of this situation by Aristotle and Machiavelli, notes their common understanding of the primacy of the political realm:

Politics—the art of living in a *polis*—is not an activity that can be dispensed with by those who prefer private life: it is not like seafaring or sculpture which those who do not wish to do so need not undertake. Political conduct is intrinsic to being a human being at a certain stage of civilization, and what it demands is intrinsic to living a successful human life.[2]

For Aristotle, as we know, a man living outside a polis must be either a beast or a god.

If the idea of necessity here does not deny the role of voluntarism, but only puts the matter in its proper place, by the same token it ought not to conjure up the image of total politics. To say that there is something necessary about politics is not to say that it is everything or the only thing. The element of necessity in politics means simply this: any satisfactory account of man's political life must recognize the existence of genuine public options, and the task of political thought is to consider how such options can be kept continually within the realm of purposeful human action. The dilemma of politics is a result not of the inexorable consequences of human action that give shape to the public, but of the fact that this necessity, this need to act, is poised against an element of indeterminism and uncertainty. This element of uncertainty is based on the fundamental observation that the existence of a public does not include the sharing of goals and purposes. This gets us away from the notion that the state is a human association with a purpose to the notion that the state is an association with a problem to which its purposes are a response. The very organization of the public in the form of the state, and the very foundation of the state in such things as loyalty, confidence, or tradition is much more a human testimony to this uncertainty than it is an articulation of some solution to the problem of ends. The public does not take on the institutions that make it a political association because of a shared view of the common good but because of the shared need to respond to certain problems. This is the source of those natural differences and conflicts that traditionally have been viewed as such essential elements of politics, and that caused Aristotle to condemn the idea of total unity derived from some intellectual certitude as not a political unity at all, but something pre-political or at least non-political. All of the various historical quests for some certitude about the ends of life and the absolutely true and good have not mitigated the problem for the man of action who is confronted with real unpredictability, real tentativeness.

Indeed, one thing that we are uncertain about is whether our uncertainty is the result of our lack of knowledge or of the utter incommensurability of the competing values of man's political life. If it is the former, then the door is open to the possibility of some ultimate end that exists "out there" to which man's historical progress is making determined strides. In such a case, the only barrier to giving politics the direction it must have is the barrier of human ignorance. Our uncertainty about action gives us, if nothing else, a sense of freedom—of man making a difference in the world —and hence the determinist pressures to offer some certainty that removes the weight of freedom and responsibility. The problem with determinism is not merely that, like other philosophical claims, it too is in the order of belief, but that it is a belief dislodged from any pragmatic grounds for testing it. Isaiah Berlin offers a typically pragmatic line of criticism:

I do not here wish to say that determinism is necessarily false, only that we neither speak nor think as if it could be true, and that it is difficult, and perhaps beyond our normal powers, to conceive what our picture of the world would be if we seriously believed it.[3]

Interestingly, V. I. Lenin, operating from a long and meticulously developed tradition of historical determinism, nevertheless had to confront, at the very moment of trying to transform his world-view into a basis for political action, the query of all men of action: What is to be done? This may seem to be a curious situation: the need to act mixed with uncertainty of purpose. But is this not the very situation Aristotle presents? Man is by nature a political animal, but his political life is beyond the realm of necessity. Is this not the setting of the Machiavellian prince, dispossessed of metaphysical truths but sensitive to the fundamental need for political action?

There are some seemingly technical exceptions to this situation. In John Locke's day, at least, it may have been possible to leave a society entirely when one was out of agreement with the direction taken by the public. However, the physical expansion of mankind and the subsequent breaking up of the whole planet into nation-states has effectively pushed Locke's alternative into the realm of imagination. Utopians of great variety have tried to keep alive the notion of organizing autonomous communities consistent with some vision of the good life. In theory at least this would mean that particular determinations of public values would enter in at the very point of origin of the community; they would not only realize that they must deal with the common condition, but they would also come together because of some shared view of how best to deal with it. This, of course, assumes—in most cases mistakenly—that the utopian community can be made immune to the indirect consequences of life beyond its narrow boundaries. Despite these technical, if not unrealistic, exceptions, the public is distinguished by its congenital lack of particular purposes and, therefore, its dependence on some other factor to hold it together. One way to appreciate this observation is to observe that when an interest group seriously quarrels over its particular purposes, a likely development is for new groups to spin off, whereas the public lives with continual quarreling that will seldom lead to a division into two publics or states, even where conflict is intense and militant. The boundaries of the state are more often rearranged by international war and diplomacy. Obviously, something aside from a shared articulate sense of purpose holds publics together; this factor may be history, culture, language, sense of nationhood, or simply force, but in a purely political sense it is the awareness, however slight, of the indirect consequences of human association and of the need to assert control over these consequences.

One other factor holds the public together and distinguishes it from private secondary groups and that is its manifestation in the form of the state. The state as a group results from what the public sees that it has to do and the state is characterized by its monopoly of violence, its rule over territory, and its effectively involuntary membership. Thus, when it is said that the public acts, there is the connotation of unanimity of goals where such unanimity is not built into the public at its origin. At this point a basic problem of the public interest is raised: How is it possible to speak of the public as taking action? At best the state takes action in everyone's name and that may be justified on the basis of some theory of contract or legitimacy, but this does not assume unanimity of the citizens. If it is assumed, quite safely, that the public will never be unanimous, then the state institution is acting on the strength of the stronger elements within the public. In such a case it is misleading, if not simply incorrect, to say that the public is acting. This does not deny that the state may have very articulately defined goals, but only that it is wrong to impute those goals to the public at large. In fact, it could be further argued that those states most clear in their purposes have also been the least popularly based, since such goals are more easily determined by a small cohesive elite capable of imposing them on society.

These comments are meant to show the distinctive problems of the behavior of the public as a group, but they also suggest a connection between the problem of the public interest and the problem of democracy. The notion that the public truly acts in more than a nominal or symbolic way would seem to be a distinctly democratic idea. The disenchantment with pure democracy as opposed to representative democracy seems to result from the apparent implausibility of an all-inclusive public effectively taking common action. Therefore, it would seem that inquiry into the possibility of realizing the determination of the public interest in a non-symbolic way is bound up with the possibility of realizing some pure notion of democracy. This is not to suggest that the public interest is an exclusively democratic idea, but it does suggest that an analysis of the operations involved in the proposition that the state speaks for the public in determining its interest may establish what is really meant in talking of the democratic form of the state. The problem of determining the public interest is the problem of determining how a segment of the public, through leadership of the state, may legitimately be said to speak for the whole public or else how the public may speak and act for itself in some way. Further, it is important not to confuse the problem of organizing the state with the problem of determining the public interest—the latter directly addresses itself to the problem of political values, to how things ought to be and to how this "ought" breathes life into the idea of authority. Thus, more precisely, the question is how the public interest can be determined authoritatively and rightly.

The problem of the public interest is that membership in the public and the problems the public faces are given while the direction that the public should take is an open question. The brute fact of shared conditions of life pushes on the members of the public a task that they may not fully be able to understand or perform and these same brute facts stand in tension to the spirit of individualism that has been so important in the modern world. It is a problem not merely of how people manage to join together behind certain values and goals, but of how they manage to do this in the face of the intransigent and inescapable fact of their shared circumstances in society. The apprehensions in such a situation are numerous and real: Will the state be guided by dogmas not open to free examination? Who will be allowed to formulate dogmas? Will there not always be dissent, and if so, what will happen to it? How will a society change its direction, once determined? Are there no ways for one to be freed of these public burdens? Does there have to be the same ruling direction for everyone? As these questions reveal, two seemingly inconsistent realities confront each other: the collective reality of the public condition and the individual reality of each man as a unique and independent thinker and actor. In the framework of such dilemmas inquiry into the determination of the public interest must proceed.

The ultimate purpose of what follows is to offer an adequate theoretical understanding of how the public good may be determined in the political life of a society. The resulting theory should provide a critical perspective from which to appraise the real world of politics as well as prevailing theories of politics. The first step will be to elaborate a pragmatic approach to the analysis of beliefs and values. The second step will be the application of this approach to the peculiar problem of the public interest.

NOTES

1. Aristotle comments that "What we do deliberate about are things that are in our power and can be realized in action; in fact, these are the only things that remain to be considered. For in addition to nature, necessity, and chance, we regard as causal principles intelligence and anything done through human agency." *Nicomachean Ethics, pp.* 60–61.
2. Isaiah Berlin, "Machiavelli," p. 23.
3. Berlin, *Four Essays on Liberty,* p. 71.

CHAPTER FIVE

THE PRAGMATIC SITUATION

What has been described is the dilemma of an identifiable public with real and inescapable collective problems but with no given direction. The argument to be considered is that the public good, the goals that are responsive to the public condition, consists of intelligible and rational objects of human action, and that in positing the public good it is possible to avoid conceiving of it either as any policy outcomes that result from acceptable political procedures or as the rationale for the preferences of people powerful enough to impose their own view of things. The assertion that the public good can be intelligently determined, analyzed, and evaluated obviously requires the establishment of some epistemological point of view about the determination of values and beliefs. In this respect the pragmatic school of thought should hopefully serve to resolve the very problems that it has assisted so far in broadly identifying.

The reason for turning to pragmatism is to find an alternative theoretical point of view from which the dilemma of the public good can be recognized and dealt with. There is a need to avoid both an absolutist solution and any solution that does not respect the needs of public life and the needs of the individual person. Pragmatism's association with liberal and progressive views of democracy and with concrete and practical modes of analysis is fairly well recognized. What is perhaps less obvious is that pragmatism goes well beyond a limited positivist view of empirical knowledge, was never comfortable with a conventional utilitarian ethics, and discovered, through the seemingly mundane concern with the practical, larger realms of truth, meaning, and value. John P. East, commenting on the relation between pragmatism and behavioralism, notes that the former is not "exclusive, intolerant, or imperialistic"; rather, it is "eclectic, inclusive, tolerant, and completely hospitable and libertarian to all approaches."[1] Further, he notes that "pragmatism is fact minded, but it is infinitely more than that. In fact, the early pragmatists explicitly rejected approaches that were *solely* scientific or empirical."[2] Thus, pragmatism encompasses many apparent tensions which, to the pragmatist's philosophical opponents, have been considered critical, though it is possible to identify an underlying clarity and consistency of approach. Among the unifying elements is a thorough commitment to the plurality of methods of inquiry, a freedom from any *a priori* views of the existential context in which man must operate, and a commitment to the search for truth that does not cede ground to the easy arrogance of the absolutist or the restrictive fetters of the skeptic—both provide whole, "intellectualist" answers that serve to close off the processes of inquiry and action and the full empirical process of verification. The eclipse of the public interest is a case in point. To understand the unique position the pragmatists have staked out and to show how their critical perspective contributes to confronting the problem at hand, it is necessary to identify and understand the roots of the pragmatic approach.

Pragmatism distinguishes itself at the very outset by the philosophical starting point to which it is committed. Charles Peirce raises the question of what state of mind one starts out with when beginning to search out truth and "dismiss make-believe." The conventional philosophical approach to this question is to assert some root principle upon which the construction of a larger system of thought depends. This root assertion may be claimed as self-evident, a universally obvious fact or proposition, but it is not susceptible to the strategies of proof finally set up by the larger system it supports. Peirce suggests a fresh alternative to the premises of the various existing schools of thought that invariably "propose that philosophy shall take its start from one or another state of mind in which no man, least of all the beginner in philosophy, actually is." He rejects the fabricated starting points of "doubt" or "immediate sense data" and proposes that there is but one state of mind from which you can "set out," namely, the very state of mind in which you actually find yourself at the time you do "set out"—a state in which you are laden with an immense mass of cognition already formed, of which you cannot divest yourself if you would, and who knows whether, if you could, you would not have made all knowledge impossible to yourself?[3]

In starting out from the point where you find yourself, you recognize that you doubt many things, but also that you already believe many things: you do not begin *tabula rasa*. Thus, the doubt upon which Peirce builds inquiry is unlike metaphysical, make-believe Cartesian doubt, for "if pedantry has not eaten all the reality out of you, [you] recognize, as you must, that there is much that you do not doubt, in the least."[4] Peirce is making a dramatic proposal, which serves to link together the world of the philosopher and the world of the man of action—without identifying the two—and opens the door to a system of thought that is relevant and human. Despite the form that philosophical inquiry later takes, is there any reason why it should not begin with the very state of mind in which the philosopher finds himself when he sets out? Is there any other starting point that is more real or about which one could feel more confident? Indeed, despite facades, is this not the invariable starting point of any philosopher, whether or not he wishes to admit it and live up to its consequences? John Dewey argues in *Reconstruction in Philosophy* that traditional philosophy had always attempted to preserve social traditions against the uncertain facts of the world and always felt the need to build its foundations outside of immediate human experience. Thus, philosophy developed as other-worldly and esoteric ("intellectualist," according to James) not only in the ultimate conclusions it reached but at the very root of its thought.[5] The starting point of pragmatism, on the contrary, suggests the need for a philosophy that may roam freely in rarefied speculation but is necessarily tied to the practical situation and needs of man. The starting point does not limit where thought can go but it establishes the point where it invariably begins and ends.

The notion that philosophy must begin within a concrete human context and be tailored to serve human needs is a dominant theme of pragmatism. William James dwells on the balance between the technical form and the practical ramifications of philosophic activity, admitting that philosophy "bakes no bread" but that, repugnant as its manners, its doubting and challenging, its quibbling and dialectics, often are to common people, no one of us can get along without the farflashing beams of light it sends over the world's perspectives,

and this should give to it "an interest that is much more than professional."[6] The philosopher "launches himself on the speculative sea," but whatever his discoveries, "the utmost result they can issue in is some new practical maxim or resolve, or the denial of some old one, with which inevitably he is sooner or later washed ashore on the *terra firma* of concrete life again."[7] James is prepared to explore the technical insofar as it can be ultimately relevant to the concrete problems of people's lives; "I risk it," he adds only half facetiously, "because the very lectures I speak of *drew* —they brought good audiences."[8]

The principle of "setting out from the point where one is when he sets out" not only establishes a concern for the practical ramifications of philosophy but also establishes that the context in which issues are raised and inquiry begins includes elements of both belief and doubt. "Doubt and Belief," explains Peirce, "designate the starting of any question, no matter how small or how great, and the resolution of it." As for the properties of belief, "First, it is something we are aware of; second, it appeases the irritation of doubt; and, third, it involves the establishment in our nature of a rule of action."[9] Poised against belief is the "irritation of doubt," which "causes a struggle to attain a state of belief" and "stimulates us to inquiry until it is destroyed."[10] The very point of "setting out" is a point at which various beliefs are already accepted and in use, but equally present are doubts that stimulate and move one to establish some basis for belief that can serve as a new guide to action. "The object of reasoning is to find out, from the consideration of what we already know, something else which we do not know,"[11] such that the movement from doubt to belief forms a process in which a belief represents both a tentative end to inquiry and the very beginning of new inquiry because of the further doubts that it generates. In a sense, belief is "thought at rest," which suggests a vibrant, fluid process moving from belief to doubt and back again, with doubt being the fillip and belief being, as Peirce so colorfully puts it, "the demicadence which closes a musical phrase in the symphony of our intellectual life."[12] Similarly, for James the movement from doubt to belief is "full of lively relief and pleasure" and is marked by a "strong feeling of ease, peace, rest."[13]

The radical consequence of this view of inquiry is stated quite bluntly by Peirce when he writes that "the most that can be maintained is, that we seek for a belief that we shall *think* to be true," so that "the settlement of opinion is the sole end of inquiry."[14] This opinion-settling view is equally asserted by James:

I will only remind you that each one of us is entitled either to doubt or believe in the harmony between his faculties and the truth; and that, whether he doubt or believe, he does it alike on his personal responsibility and risk.[15]

The reasons why and how such a view avoids being solipsistic and does not deny objective reality are of the essence of the pragmatic view of the meaning of truth.[16] What this view is intended to avoid is an *a priori* commitment to some "first truth" and a subsequent fixed scheme of proof. What we believe, we assert to be true. The whole point of beliefs is that in some way or other we are satisfied with them, and if that is the case, why are they not sufficient as a basis on which to build further inquiry? If one is insecure about their character as "mere opinion," then doubts are raised about them, but doubt must be alive and actual; the purpose and stimulus to inquiry comes directly from the concrete state of doubting. The opinion-settling view is a blend of frankness, realism, hope, and confidence; rather than encouraging a cynicism of human rationality, it prepares the ground for constructively and optimistically confronting exactly what is at stake in human thought. It abhors static and pretentious recipes for proof and certitude and turns to processes of inquiry rooted in the human condition, which aid the precarious, risky business of thinking clearly and rationally. For pragmatism, as will be seen, the real test of beliefs is that men must live with them.

Since inquiry into the soundness of beliefs is stirred by actual doubt, not abstract questioning, it is possible to speak of a field of awareness of experiences that constitutes the "interest" or "attention" of the investigator. James writes:

It is by the interest and importance that experiences have for us, by the emotions they excite, and the purposes they subserve, by their effective values, in short, that their consecution in our several conscious streams, as "thoughts" of ours, is mainly ruled.[7]

Earlier it was seen that James used the "liveness" of an option, one's interest or stake in it, to determine the impact of a particular matter of inquiry and choice. The importance of this matter of interest and attention is that it distinguishes the pragmatic viewpoint from abstract empiricism. "The likenesses and differences that we observe in facts are not merely thrust upon us without our consent or connivance," explains Josiah Royce. "They are the objects of our attentive interest."[18] The whole bundle of facts in the world are not simply given as such; rather, out of man's interaction with the world, certain facts are attended to and others ignored, and this determination is bound up with man's purposefulness and may result from an act of his will. In a sense, "the fact observed is the fulfillment of our intent to observe that kind of fact."[19] The facts of the world are not encountered

. . . wholly apart from any of our specific purposes, but correlative to certain tendencies of our will, i.e. to certain interests, which are fulfilled in recognizing these specific sorts of likenesses and differences which we come to observe.[20]

Royce further elaborates on this theme of how men go out to meet the facts by distinguishing between the foreground and the background of knowledge: the former representing objects of attention that we observe and the latter being "the rest of the universe." The background is acknowledged by the admission that there is the rest of the world beyond the things one has attended to and the rest of the world is consequential even though we have not grasped it like the foreground of our knowledge. "Our finitude means, then, an actual inattention—a lack of successful interests, at this conscious instant, in more than a very few details of the universe,"[21] and this "theory of our relations, as finite knowers, to the real world, predetermines what form we ascribe to the system of facts whose reality we acknowledge."[22] The things one attends to, his interest, his purpose in inquiry, the foreground of his knowledge, and the theories he uses to order the world are all interrelated in the pragmatic situation, the situation of setting out in the state of mind in which one finds oneself at the moment. The pragmatic situation, with the irritation of actual doubt and the formation of our attention, serves to explain why certain facts are dealt with over other facts and why particular theories develop over other theories.

The context of inquiry established by the pragmatists thus

consists of an existential starting point, the structuring of the investigation around actual beliefs and doubts that are present, and the foreground of experience, one's interest, that makes knowledge finite. At this point a couple of observations should be made about the pragmatic context of inquiry. The first concerns the relationship that is established between theoretical and practical concerns, which parallels the earlier distinction between theoretical ideas and ideas-in-use. For pragmatists, theoretical concerns derive from the practical but are not bound tight or limited by the practical. The actual and the concrete, including, e.g., ideas-in-use, represent the beginning and the end of a theoretical task, the point from which it gets launched and the point to which it must return. This means that the relation between the theoretical and the practical, the concrete underpinning of theory, will be measured by payoffs, not by methods. This allows for a much broader conception of realism in which the theorist, though ultimately terminating his speculations in the practical, is set free to push beyond the immediate foreground, the immediate finite conceptions of practicality. The pragmatist is trying to set the stage for theoretical activity that is truly realistic but effectively critical, thus bridging the historical gap between an idealism that views the practical with disdain and a realism that creates a deadening lack of self-examination.

The other observation is that in introducing the grounds of their philosophic approach, the pragmatists do not restrict themselves to issues of fact over value. Indeed, at the outset they do not even make the distinction. Thus, in approaching the issue of how beliefs are fixed and settled, the presumption is that these may be beliefs about what *is* or about what *ought to be*. Also, by keeping the question open, the pragmatist allows for a wide range of forms that beliefs take, forms that would be pushed to the background by an exaggerated emphasis on the is/ought dichotomy: beliefs about what will, or could, or might be. However, the fact/value distinction is not eliminated altogether and how it fits into the pragmatic outlook will be shown later.

The essentials of pragmatism consist of an accounting of how man moves from a condition of doubt to a condition of belief. In the concrete experience of living with beliefs and doubts, man searches for some basis on which to believe—not to believe anything in any way, but to believe securely, with confidence that the belief will not crumble immediately upon being grasped. One way of putting this is to say that man wants to believe the truth. Charles Peirce reviews the various inadequate ways that men try to fix their beliefs—out of pure tenaciousness, a stubborn isolation from anything that might make one question his beliefs; by some established social power which assures through its punitiveness that a set of doctrines will be held secure; or by being part of a system resting on *a priori* propositions that seem somehow reasonably tenable. All such methods of belief have played their role in history and they all share certain common deficiencies.[23] What their various deficiencies amount to is the absence of the element of real experience, for man "should consider that, after all, he wishes his opinions to coincide with the facts, and that there is no reason why the results of those three first methods should do so."[24] The only method that offers the possibility of such coincidence is an experimental method of scientific investigation through which objective reality enters into the very processes of forming opinions. This does not mean that the known techniques of science hereby become the measure of the true and the rational, but these techniques do suggest ways of getting at reality; whereas tenaciousness, authority, and *a priori* rationalism are attempts to arrive at some point of belief without ever reaching out to experience.

The question of how we get at reality and how this leads to beliefs that can somehow be considered more or less true brings the discussion to the very heart of the pragmatist point of view, to what may be called the pragmatic principle. Though stated in various forms, the principle roughly amounts to this: in saying that such and such a belief is true (whether it be a "fact" or a "value"), what is meant is only that the belief identifies certain real consequences and effects that work and are satisfying. For example, if A and B both have the consequence C and no other consequence, then there is no truth to the belief in a distinction between A and B because such a belief would be dissatisfying. The search for a consequence other than C would be unfulfilled, and the only belief that would work would be one that saw A and B leading to C. "Our idea of anything *is* our idea of its sensible effects," according to Peirce, and this accounts for the meaning of our ideas:

Consider what effects, that might conceivably have practical bearings, we conceive the object of our perception to have. Then our conception of these effects is the whole of our conception of the object.[25]

In the pursuit of truth we then look to see that the expected effects that were pointed to take place, that the conception worked and satisfies the purposes that put us on the trail of inquiry.

What Peirce means here by "sensible effects" is much broader than the notion of an immediate empirical referent. Consider how the pragmatic principle applies to cases where sense data are presumably deceiving us. Let us say that there is a bucket of water with a pole stuck into it and because of its position in the water the pole appears bent. An observer who comes upon the scene looking for a straight pole identifies the pole in the water as what he wants, takes it out and uses it. The belief he establishes for himself, that "the pole over there in the bucket of water is straight," is confirmed not immediately by sense data but by the act of removing the pole from the water and discovering that his belief produced satisfying results, i.e., a usable straight pole. Thus, the statement of belief that the pole is straight could be translated to mean that "believing that the pole is straight will lead to the satisfying consequences (sensible effects) of discovering that it is straight when I remove it from the bucket." The concept of "straightness" could not be said to have an empirical referent in the form of sense data presented to an uninvolved observer, for the data would seem immediately to suggest a bent pole; the referent, in fact, consists of the effects that *will* result when the belief in the pole's straightness is confirmed through action.

Summarizing Peirce, James explains that "the pragmatic method . . . is to try to interpret each notion by tracing its respective practical consequences."[26] Such a method, by operating within the pragmatic situation and by depending on the effects of things, means "that our beliefs are really rules for action," and "to develop a thought's meaning, we need only determine what conduct it is fitted to produce: that conduct is for us its sole significance."[27] Having formed conceptions in this way, the truth of ideas is measured "just in so far as they help us to get into satisfactory relations with other parts of our experience."[28] Thus, conceptions identify nothing more than "effects"—that is their full significance—and their truth depends on whether or not they work. This is the distinctive mark of the pragmatist's commitment: it is a commitment to the "cash-value" of beliefs, to their relevance to human activity and purpose. Needless to say, this proposal of the pragmatists is sufficiently dramatic to invite the greatest of controversies and, in fact, most of James's writing after the publication of *Pragmatism* was concerned with confronting the reaction to it. The virulence of the reaction was in no small part caused by the candidness of his statements about the expediency and workability of truth. As we sort out the problems raised by the pragmatic principle, the writing of James will be heavily emphasized to make the exposition more manageable, since James has essentially distilled the views of Dewey, Peirce, and others in his own presentation, which represents the fullest expression of the pragmatic approach.

NOTES

1. John P. East, p. 603.
2. East, p. 604.
3. Charles S. Peirce, *Philosophical Writings of Peirce*, p. 256.
4. Peirce, p. 256.
5. John Dewey, *Reconstruction in Philosophy.*
6. William James, *Pragmatism*, p. 19.
7. William James, *The Will to Believe*, p. 143. Josiah Royce, even though drawing out the idealistic side of pragmatism, observes in regard to the problems of metaphysics that "their significance for the whole business of every man ought to be immediately obvious, unless indeed the philosopher who expounds them has failed in his task." Josiah Royce, *The World and the Individual*, Vol. II, p. 1. He adds to this the typically pragmatic assertion that "the practical good sense of mankind is to be respected when it demands that the solitary labors of the seeker for truth shall in the end be submitted . . . to the social and ethical judgment of practical men." Royce, p. 3.
8. James, *Pragmatism*, p. 18.
9. Peirce, pp. 26–28; see also Dewey, *Reconstruction*, p. 138.
10. Peirce, p. 10.
11. Peirce, p. 7.
12. Peirce, pp. 28–29.
13. James, *Will to Believe*, p. 63.
14. Peirce, pp. 10–11.
15. James, *Will to Believe*, pp. 116–117.
16. The issue of the objectivity and subjectivity of the pragmatist's view of truth will be sorted out in Chapter VI, but for the specific response of James to the charge of solipsism see William James, *The Meaning of Truth*, pp. 212–216; see also William James, *Essays in Radical Empiricism*, Chapter 9.
17. James, *Radical Empiricism*, p. 151.
18. Josiah Royce, *World and Individual*, p. 48.
19. Royce, p. 50.
20. Royce, pp. 60–51.
21. Royce, p. 59; se also Royce, pp. 53–56.
22. Royce, p. 62.
23. Peirce, pp.12–18.
24. Peirce, p. 21.
25. Peirce, p. 31.
26. James, *Pragmatism*, p. 42.
27. James, *Pragmatism*, p. 43.
28. James, *Pragmatism*, p. 49.

CHAPTER SIX

KNOWING AND ACTING

The notion that the truth is something workable and satisfying is a good point on which to begin clearing up the significance of the pragmatic principle. An obvious line of criticism is that such a notion leads to the conclusion that truth is nothing more than subjective convenience, whatever pleases one's fancy, and that it is only established by the most mundane measure of utility. To appreciate what the pragmatist is saying—and why it is none of these things— it is important to consider why anyone is concerned about the truth in the first place. Why is it so important that our beliefs be true? If truth means a correspondence between idea and object, why do men seek such correspondence? For one thing, without it all our experience will go awry. Whether or not it is true that the bus is scheduled to arrive at eleven o'clock makes a difference, and if every day we wait for it at twelve o'clock and it never comes and we never get where we want to go at twelve o'clock, we will not be very satisfied with our belief; we will begin to have some doubts. Thus, "The payments true ideas bring are the sole why of our duty to follow them."[1] The truth is desired for what it does, and is true because its results meet the expectations it raises. For someone who never travels on buses, the truth about the time a bus arrives has no meaning aside from the possibility of testing the truth. This is not to say that people do not collect random and useless pieces of information, but it does mean that their merit as being true only results from, and can only be known through, their satisfying effects. The pragmatic principle thus derives directly from having a purpose to know the truth, a purpose that comes from the existential configuration of our doubts and beliefs. James does not deny that ideas should "agree," for that is the very terminus of the search for the truth,[2] but he does ask how we know that there is such agreement and he answers that

to "agree" in the widest sense with a reality can only mean to be guided straight up to it or into its surroundings, or to be put into such working touch with it as to handle either it or something connected with it better than if we disagreed.[3]

Agreements are arrived at not only because they work, because experience confirms the connection between the idea and the object, but also because what is fully meant by this true relation of idea and object is captured in its "working." To assert that the elements "agree" independently of this "working" arrangement is a closed abstraction that "makes no difference to reality itself; it is supervenient, inert, static, a reflection merely."[4] Purpose, therefore, is intimately bound up with knowing because it is the vehicle for positing that things do "agree" and for establishing the reasons why the agreement is sought after. "Truth" that is claimed to be separate from purposes worked out in experience is divorced from the opportunity to test it.

What may be confusing is how the view that beliefs "appear true only because they work satisfactorily"[5] is related to some measure of practicality. Many misunderstandings of pragmatism have resulted from a narrow interpretation of terms. The satisfaction that truth gives is not limited to an immediate utility or to practicality in the conventional sense. The way truth works may be a long, drawn out process with no quickly identifiable "payoff." The inevitable practical issue behind any inquiry may be "conjectural and remote" and the outcomes "delicate and distant."[6] The practical framework of inquiry only establishes the point from which inquiry sets out and the ultimate point that it may reach. The intervening process may involve great digression, wandering, and speculation over matters that have little, on the face of it, to do with our daily lives; and this is why pragmatism "so far from keeping her eyes on the immediate practical foreground, as she is accused of doing, dwells just as much upon the world's remotest perspectives."[7] Real effects and consequences are not necessarily immediate; they may lurk in the background, they may be off in the future or they may be only potential at the moment, but in relation to them our ideas must work. Though James's terminology—"payoffs," "cash-value"—may have contributed much to misunderstanding of this point, pragmatism clearly goes beyond any immediate, measurable utility.

What distinguishes pragmatism from mere devotion to practical wisdom is that it calls into question the very rules of practicality themselves, and sees them as situational and changeable. Technically, there is a crucial difference between saying that someone is being practical and that someone is being pragmatic. Practicality is an immediate and short-run guide, which fails to question the potentiality of things; pragmatism opens the question of what will work in the widest sense and sees possibilities beyond what is immediately defined as possible. Where practicality suggests dealing with the world on its own terms, pragmatism sees those terms as man-made and alterable; practicality tells us what does work, pragmatism considers what will work or might work. This leads to an irony for those who have misunderstood the pragmatist: to be pragmatic may be highly impractical.

The truth results from a process of verification that focuses on more than immediate, instantaneous connections. Numerous intermediaries between idea and object form something like a chain of satisfying results. The function of the truth is to lead one from experience to experience, to search out the interconnections that work among various experiences, to take thought from the foreground to the background and from the known to the unknown. Rather than being a step-by-step recipe, the pragmatic process of verification works on the metaphor of a searching activity that attempts to close in on the truth so as to finally, at the end, touch it. The search consists of a whole bundle of activities that link up experiences successfully, and thoughts guide the activity successfully until and unless reality bumps up against this movement, redirects it, and makes it change course. The process of getting to the thing known occurs by "an outer chain of physical or mental intermediaries connecting thought and thing," so that "to know an object is here to lead to it through a context which the world supplies."[8] James elaborates an example of verification in which he has an idea of a particular building and is trying to show that "certain extrinsic phenomena, special exepriences of conjunction, are what impart to the image, be it what it may, its knowing office."[9] He describes what it would be like to work out the idea to its payoff:

. . . if I can lead you to the hall, and tell you of its history and present uses; if in its presence I feel my idea, however imperfect it may have been, to have led hither and to be now *terminated,* if the associates of the image and of the felt hall run parallel, so that each term of the one context corresponds serially, as I walk, with an answering term of the other; why then my soul was prophetic, and my idea must be, and by common consent would be, called cognizant of reality. That percept was what I *meant,* for into it my idea has passed by conjunctive experiences of sameness and fulfilled intention. Nowhere is there jar, but every later moment continues and corroborates an earlier one.

In this continuing and corroborating, taken in no transcendental sense, but denoting definitely felt transitions, *lies all that the knowing of a percept by an idea can possibly contain or signify.* Wherever such transitions are felt, the first experience *knows* the last one. Where they do not, or where even as possibles they can not, intervene, there can be no pretense of knowing. In this latter case the extremes will be connected, if connected at all, by inferior relations—bare likenesses or succession, or by "withness" alone. Knowledge of sensible realities thus comes to life inside the tissue of experience. It is *made;* and made by relations that unroll themselves in time. Whenever certain intermediaries are given, such that, as they develop towards their terminus, there is experience from point to point of one direction followed, and finally of one process fulfilled, the result is that *their starting-point thereby becomes a knower and their terminus an object meant or known.* That is all that knowing (in the simple case considered) can be known-as, that is the whole of its nature, put into experiential terms.[10]

This illustration should show more particularly what is meant by such phrases as "getting into 'touch' with it (reality) by innumerable paths of verification,"[11] and "growth of a mass of verification-experience,"[12] and "pieces of substantive experience, with conjunctively transitional experiences between,"[13] and "a procession of mental associates and motor consequences that follow on the thought."[14] On its face, such a process may appear cumbersome, indirect, and muddled; and, in a sense, this is all true. Since the pragmatist views method with permissiveness and tolerance, he is not prepared to set up method as a set of instructions. What fixes the method, what gives it its form and shape, is the bundle of experiences that guide and terminate it and reveal the connections in reality itself; the value of the method—it seems almost tautological to say it—is purely instrumental. There are many ways to the truth and the best one is the one that gets us there.

There is a critical difference between this view of the verification process and a constricted view of operationalism in social sicence in that the pragmatist opens the possibility, if not actually the need, to transcend immediate experience. In fact, the very process of knowing includes reaching out beyond the foreground so that there is a distinction in the process between "direct acquaintance" and "knowledge about."

Where direct acquaintance is lacking, "knowledge about" is the next best thing, and an acquaintance with what actually lies about the object, and is most closely related to it, puts such knowledge within our grasp.[15]

Most knowledge is "knowledge about" that is not completed or verified but has meaning in that "the known is a *possible* experience either of that subject or another, to which the said conjunctive transactions *would* lead, if sufficiently prolonged."[16] The "virtual knower" is one who has knowledge about, knowledge which is but a shorthand for real "acquaintance," and for which it should be able to be substituted. Such knowledge may also consist of beliefs that have accumulated at the point of setting out on an inquiry to the extent that real doubt has not yet arisen about its workability.[17] Thus, knowledge gets beyond the immediate things present by the transitions and connections in experience. On the contrary, a constricted operationalism, by resting on the immediate correspondence between thought and object, sees the foreground as the universe; and, though within the field of attention ideas operate successfully,

. . . what meets expediently all the experience in sight won't necessarily meet all farther experiences equally satisfactorily. Experience, as we know, has ways of *boiling over,* and making us correct our present formulas.[18]

Ironically, though the pragmatist has suffered under the criticism of being thoroughly subjective, James nevertheless introduces the broader continuities of objective reality as a corrective to the almost solipsistic view of operationalism. Equally ironic, the very plurality and changeableness of reality makes existing "operational" concepts often seem trivial and tautological, and this among other things leads James to call his view "radical empiricism," in contrast to the empiricism he finds in vogue. Thus, an idea does not refer simply to that which is present to the observer but to that which may be, or could be, or will be present. A narrow operationalism brings one to neither the full truth nor to satisfactory conceptions; in the former it fails because the terminus of a "chain of workings" is beyond present experiences, and in the latter it fails by excluding the possibilities that are out of its immediate reach and that necessarily affect the workability of its concepts.

The earlier critical discussion of the various ways the public interest concept has been treated was not meant to suggest the abandonment of operational concepts but rather the need to reconsider what is meant when we say "operational." It is much too narrow and constricted a view to demand that an operational concept consist of identifiable testing devices that conform to known empirical referents. Just such a constricted view leads to the suggestion that the "public interest" cannot be operationalized because the political phenomena under study do not display any collective social will. By requiring that a concept be nothing more than a "copy" of facts (directly acquainted with), the notion of a test seems superfluous. The function of the test presumably is to move from the known to the unknown, from doubt to belief, which would be redundant if the process of getting concepts is itself such a test. Experience suggests and offers ideas but it does not give them to us all filled out, settled, and refined. Correctly speaking, an "operational" concept is one about which the full truth is not known, its full corresponding reality not apparent; if it were fully true and workable it would be a terminus to the activity of inquiry, in which case the important issue would be not how to use it in research but how it was acquired in the first place. Ideas should tell us about what could be or might be not for the mere delight of dealing with the hypothetical and the imaginative but for telling about objective reality that is "out of sight" but consequential. Thus pragmatists, in using operational terms, mean quite literally ideas that operate, that are literally put to work; and as the word suggests, an operational concept is dynamic, it moves thought. The notion of operational concepts as involving a test is typically thought to mean, as Abraham Kaplan describes it, that "to each concept there corresponds a set of operations involved in its scientific use. To know these operations is to understand the concept as fully as science requires. . . ."[19] Though pragmatism considers the testing experience essential, it contends that the meaning of an idea consists not of the operations themselves but of the payoffs that result. Many different operations may lead to the same sensible effects, which would mean, according to the pragmatic principle, that there is no meaningful difference among the operations. Is the contention then among different operational conceptions perhaps phony and misleading?

Aside from the problem of how to get at the truth, which requires a broader view of operationalism, what exactly is meant by the truth and what is its character? The distinction between reality and truth is basic: "Truths emerge from facts. . . . The 'facts' themselves meanwhile are not *true*. They simply *are*. Truth is the function of the beliefs that start and terminate among them."[20] Thus James explains:

Should we ever reach absolutely terminal experiences, experiences in which we all agreed, which were superseded by no revised continuations, these would not be *true*, they would be *real*, they would simply *be*. . . . Only such *other* things as led to these by satisfactory conjunctions would be "true." Satisfactory connection of some sort with such termini is all that the word "truth" means.[21]

Thoughts, then, are the connecting links that permit one to move about experience in fruitful ways. These connections are the fluid of the verification process; they are altered by their leading to new facts, and their particular configuration is the result of our field of consciousness. In this sense theories can be said to be perspectives on phenomena that are more or less valuable, rather than more or less true in the correspondence sense.

In relation to gaining insights into the problem of the public good, two aspects of truth are important. First, the process of verification basically consists of real, consequential action; and second, the truths arrived at, the web of connections among experience, take on the character of objective reality. In the understanding of these two points Dewey's commitment to "creative intelligence" becomes meaningful. The first point means that we create facts and the second means that one of the facts we create is our own thought. The link in pragmatism between knowing and acting should already be somewhat apparent; the two are mutually interconnected in the process of relieving doubt and discovering workable beliefs. The controlled laboratory experiment is a useful substitution for the ultimate test of human action and purpose; the verification process is more correctly seen as experiential rather than experimental. "The most striking feature of the new theory," explains Peirce, reflecting on the development of pragmatism, "was its recognition of an inseparable connection between rational cognition and rational purpose."[22] The connection is that belief "involves the establishment in our nature of a rule of action,"[23] and in the process of thinking, "we come down to what is tangible and conceivably practical, . . . and there is no distinction of meaning so fine as to consist in anything but a possible difference of practice."[24] The process of knowing grows out of and feeds back into the purposes that guide activity, and human action includes the real test of our beliefs. The larger implication of this pragmatic proposition is that much of what is known is created by the knower; not only is action the essential test of reality, but it makes up reality. In relation to reality the human element is additive; and two things are added,[25] the first being "the new facts which men add to the matter of reality by the acts of their own lives."[26] There is nothing very mysterious in this, since we live in a world pervasively shaped by human action; the facts of everyday life are facts of man's creation. But what is ignored by this obvious situation is its relation to human thought. If truth means what is workable and satisfying, then positing the truth is not a mere question of searching out corresponding facts but of possibly creating a particular relation. The search for "agreement" may modify not only the idea but also the object, in which case the knower does not simply find the truth, but actually makes the truth by adding to objective reality.

What is perhaps less obvious is not only that man creates new facts but that he adds, in the knowing process, the very truths he arrives at to the sum of human experience. Therefore, the second human additive is that, in relation to reality, "what is *true of it* seems from first to last to be largely a matter of our own creation,"[27] such that it may be impossible "to separate the real from the human factors in the growth of our cognitive experience."[28] Both true and false ways of putting reality together are plural. Many sets of continuities and connections among experiences will work and each represents a different way of carving up reality. There is a double choice—between the true and the false, and between truths—and each choice comes down to human will and purpose. The way reality is conceived of is a matter of human creation and will guide the kinds of new facts that are added. Thus, James summarizes:

We add, both to the subject and predicate part of reality. The world stands really malleable, waiting to receive its final touches at our hands. . . . Man engenders truth upon it.[29]

In the thinking process, concepts have the dual character of being subjective and objective, and in the former sense they may be encountered and dealt with as our perceptions are.[30] This is why James contends that "truth here is a relation, not of our ideas to non-human realities, but of conceptual parts of our experience to sensational parts."[31] This means that the sensational parts may be made up not only of material things but of truth that is established such that "the truth which the conforming experience embodies may be a positive addition to the previous reality, and later judgments may have to conform to *it*."[32]

Again, to some extent, this notion is not thoroughly new; for example, though the public good has been considered unreal, what people think the public good is may be a relevant subject for investigation. When society is studied, the object of inquiry is not only what is happening but what people think is (or might be, or should be) happening. Though this view is commonplace enough, what pragmatism attempts to make clear is that "what people think" is two-sided, both objective and subjective, and that both sides are efficacious. One part of our sensations is working on the other parts at the very time we are examining it; concepts, as objects, are not like dead matter for they are the working of other minds. Thus, the knowledge/action relationship is not only working in the individual observer but is equally at work in the "sensational parts" that he is examining. Again, a correspondence theory of knowing may suggest that thought and objective reality be set up against each other to see if they match, but the creative power of thought which grows from its relation with action means that the process of matching misconstrues what is actually taking place, because it reflects no understanding that the two sides of the match are constantly in flux because of their interaction. The process of verifying beliefs about the world inevitably leads to forming, shaping, and adding something to reality; we verify beliefs by acting on them and by acting on them we may help to make them true. Thus, "truth *happens* to an idea. It *becomes* true, is *made* true by events. Its verity *is* in fact an event, a process."[33] As Sidney Hook puts it, for pragmatists "an idea is virtually a plan of action."[34]

All of this discussion greatly depends on an appreciation of the relation between knowing and acting. Though the context of actual beliefs and doubts that identify a purpose behind knowing—the stimulus to relieve the irritation of doubt—aids the relationship between knowing and acting, it only becomes a clearly dependent relation through the process of verification. Since beliefs, as something like hypotheses, stand for working arrangements among our experiences, their verification must fall back on practice. Where the need to know is compelling and where the substitutional activity of the controlled experiment does not suit, the truth becomes more than a possible guide to action; rather, it becomes posited only through consequential action. Activity follows out the chain of connections in experience and puts one really in touch with things; this puts one in the position of using mere "knowledge about" something as the only vehicle for getting in "direct acquaintance" with it and thereby causes us to act "as if" such-and-such were true. The idea that we act "as if" something were true results from the fact that our ideas do not merely copy reality but are meant to work for us, to put us in touch with facts immediately out of reach. "Knowledge about" is meaningful because it works and because of where it takes us, and it takes us places because it is acted upon, and by the efficacy of this action there may be created the very reality that was earlier presumed.

One problem raised by the relationship between knowing and acting is whether or not the acting should be conceived of in terms of controlled laboratory experimentation or in terms of the test of concrete life experience. The pragmatist surely wishes to include the latter, though the physical sciences have dwelt on the development of controlled experimentation. This gives the impression of an easy compartmentalizing of "pure" and "applied" activities, a separation of knowing from implications about larger purposes. The pragmatic response is that even the activities of "pure" research are set within some configuration of motivations, purposes, beliefs, and doubts. But even further, pragmatism suggests why the social and behavioral sciences, at least, cannot depend upon or limit themselves to controlled experimentation. The reason can be found in the consequences of those "additive elements" mentioned above, combined with the idea of the two levels of meaning involved in social inquiry. Man not only "makes things true" but the truth itself becomes part of sensational experience. Therefore, in setting up a testing situation, an "experiment" may require real purposes and real action, unleashing real consequences, which will allow for not merely examining the hypothesis but for examining the concrete effects of taking a believing attitude toward the hypothesis. One might ask: Is x true? To what extent will my action make x true (1st additive)? To what extent will my belief that x is true help to confirm the truth of x (2nd additive)? Is this belief as the source of concrete commitment and action precisely the element that cannot be given any controlled, laboratory reconstruction? The verification process itself denies any easy, comfortable division between the search for truth on the one hand and purposeful social and political action on the other. When those purposes happen to be set in the framework of genuine options, the two concerns are almost inextricable.

What the pragmatist rejects, then, is any static dichotomy between Thinking and Acting; rather the processes of intellect and will are tied together in the incessant and interconnected human activities of knowing, believing, creating, corroborating, testing, and hoping. Man has no limit and no restriction, unless it is the very bottom of what is possible, some ultimate terminus where his will, his creations, and the brute facts of given reality converge in some fully satisfying order. Short of that, the pragmatist will be guided by the fittings, workings, and successes that his ideas have and will refuse to be hampered by any fixed formula or *a priori* commitment. Most important of all is that this approach, rather than limiting our vision to the mundane and practical, equips us, in the most realistic way, to explore remote and distant human possibilities, to make sense of the past so as to know what we will be doing in the future instead of thinking of both past and future as the dark side of the moon. In the simplest sense, of course, pragmatism is a humanist doctrine which sees man as the measure and which sees other philosophical viewpoints as attempts to remove knowledge from the human condition, to dehumanize and thereby to make it alien. The workings of human thought do not constitute a *sanctum sanctorum* but are open to all who will attend to the concretely human problems raised by the search for truth.

NOTES

1. William James, *Pragmatism,* p. 150.
2. William James, *The Meaning of Truth,* pp. 156–157. Though pragmatism asserts that there is objective reality, the so-called "agreement" of thoughts with it is still unlike a process of copying or reflecting the thing in our mind. Dewey explains that, "We do not measure the worth or reality of the tool by its closeness to its natural prototypes, but by its efficiency in

doing its work." John Dewey, *Essays in Experimental Logic*, p. 56. Truth is thus and instrument, an expedient of our thinking, and is measured by what it does; if a correspondence takes place, it is like the correspondence of a key to a lock. See Sidney Hook, pp. 154–155; also see James, *Meaning*, pp. 78–82.

3. James, *Pragmatism*, p. 140.
4. James, *Pragmatism*, p. 147.
5. James, *Meaning*, p. 240.
6. James, *Pragmatism*, pp. 73–74. When James refers to expediency, he means "expedient in almost any fashion; and expedient in the long run on the whole of course." James, *Pragmatism*, p. 145.
7. James, *Pragmatism*, p. 86.
8. James, *Meaning*, p. 86.
9. James, *Meaning*, p. 104.
10. James, *Meaning*, pp. 105–106.
11. James, *Meaning*, p. 214.
12. James, *Pragmatism*, p. 146.
13. James, *Meaning*, p. 107.
14. James, *Meaning*, pp. 44–45.
15. James, *Meaning*, p. 119.
16. James, *Meaning*, p. 103.
17. James, *Meaning*, pp. 113–115.
18. James, *Pragmatism*, p. 145.
19. Abraham Kaplin, p. 40.
20. James, *Pragmatism*, p. 147; see also James, *Meaning*, p. 155.
21. James, *Meaning*, p. 134.
22. Charles S. Peirce, *Philosophical Writings of Peirce*, pp. 252–253.
23. Peirce, p. 28.
24. Peirce, p. 30.
25. Dewey describes the two additives as the double effects of a reflection: 1) "Its immediate outcome is . . . the direct reorganization of a situation" and 2) "Its indirect and intellectual product is the defining of a meaning which . . . is a resource in subsequent investigation." John Dewey, *Essays in Experimental Logic*, p. 58.
26. James, *Pragmatism*, p. 162; James admits his view is subjectivist to the extent that "inasmuch as it treats the thinker as being himself one portion of reality, it must also allow that some of the realities that he declares for true are created by his being there." William James, *Essays in Radical Empiricism*, p. 251.
27. James, *Pragmatism*, p. 166.
28. James, *Pragmatism*, p. 163.
29. James, *Pragmatism*, p. 167.
30. See James, *Radical Empiricism*, pp. 9–16.
31. James, *Meaning*, p. 82.
32. James, *Meaning*, p. 101.
33. James, *Pragmatism*, p. 133.
34. Hook, p. 152.

CHAPTER SEVEN

ANALYTICAL ROOTS
OF THE PROBLEM

What is to be made of this philosophy of pragmatism? This approach seems at once so skeptical and iconoclastic, yet so soft-headed and naive; it seems so subjective at its roots, yet so confident of the power of objective, concrete reality to steer man correctly through his experiences; it offers so little to grasp firmly in the quest for certain reliable knowledge, no set method, no set first truth. And what is the end result: settling our beliefs in a world where so much philosophy has dedicated itself to condemning mere opinion? Is that the terminus, to think that what we believe is true? How do we apply this to the problems of social inquiry?

What can be said of the public good at this point is that it is nothing more or less than a particular kind of belief, a belief that represents the terminus of the process by which the public verifies its ideas about how to control and regulate indirect social consequences or, more particularly, all of the conclusions along the way that are found workable and satisfying. On the surface it may appear that the discussion has not come very far if it has only come to this. But though this formulation may not seem terribly revealing about what the public good is, it may be quite helpful in telling what the public good *is not*. The first payoff of this pragmatic formulation should be to clear away the underbrush of false issues and help to redirect inquiry.

The main impediment that pragmatism clears out of the path of inquiry is what James calls "vicious abstractionism."[1] This abstractionism, or petrifaction of ideas, manifests itself in much discussion over the public good. Briefly, what happens is that important and salient characteristics of phenomena are used to make mental constructs. These constructs are extremely valuable as substitutions or mental shorthand, which is the sense in which the pragmatist takes them. What tends to happen, however, is that these concepts, rather than being handy vehicles for guiding us through our experiences, become fixed and arrested meanings. They no longer partake of the nuance and richness of the experiences with which they are intended to put us in touch. James, in fact, sees such abstractionism as the critical weakness of his opponents:

Abstraction, functioning in this way, becomes a means of arrest far more than a means of advance in thought. It mutilates things; it creates difficulties and finds impossibilities; and more than half the trouble that metaphysicians and logicians give themselves over the paradoxes and dialectical puzzles of the universe may, I am convinced, be traced to this relatively simple source.[2]

A case in point are the abstractions "fact" and "value," which have had such an effect on the course of contemporary political inquiry. What impresses one about facts, spoken of in the abstract, is their "brute" character that makes them fairly fixed, somehow "out there" and open for all to encounter in some common way. The feeling is that facts, by virtue of a certain independence from man that objective reality possesses, can be known with some confidence and this knowledge can be shared. Values, on the other hand, seem bound up with human will, which is individualized and has no fixed existence independent of man; in seeking to share and rightly determine values, there is nothing outside of man that we can lean against. Various characteristics of facts and values such as these are accumulated and form some conception, hopefully a useful conception, of how "is" and "ought" statements, respectively, work. However, when the petrifaction of these abstractions sets in, the realm of facts may begin to appear thoroughly unmalleable and lacking in any human element and the realm of values begins to appear thoroughly relative and capricious. Further, the supposed firmness, bruteness, and objectiveness of the facts may become a standard for determining values in a utilitarian way, or one may be pushed to search out some Absolute Value that will be as secure and fixed as the presumed world of hard facts. What might have been a useful distinction develops into rigid categories that put values out of reach of human rationality or into the realm of fixed ideals, give a false impression of the static character of objective reality, and ignore the ubiquitous interrelation of the two realms of facts and values.

Such vicious abstractionism has led to the notion that making sense of the public good requires nothing short of proving the truth and rightness, once and for all, of some Public Good or, for that matter, providing some method for discovering the Public Good that is as secure and reliable as the methods of science. The false problem that comes from putting the issue in these terms is caused by petrifaction in the viewpoint of scientific method and empirical knowledge. The search for the Public Good has been unproductive, but no more so than would be the search for Objective Reality or Scientific Method. By avoiding such abstractionism, it is possible to appreciate that though "sensations are forced upon us, coming we know not whence," we nevertheless "still have freedom in our dealings with them."[3] Similarly, though values are relative, there may be impressive continuities in the development of human values that deny the petrified concept of values as something indeterminate. The radical empirical approach of pragmatism makes no presumptions about the distinction between facts and values and finds their meaning fully presented not in the conceptual shorthands but in the way they allow one to deal successfully with actual human experiences. As William James would have the distinction: " 'The True,' to put it very briefly, is only the expedient in the way of our thinking, just as the 'right' is only the expedient in the way of our behaving."[4] Indeed, James pursues this train of thought to the conclusion that "truth is *one species of good,* and not, as is usually supposed, a category distinct from good, and co-ordinate with it. The true is the name of whatever proves itself to be good in the way of belief. . . ."[5] The belief in a fact/value dichotomy, which sees values as subjective and undemonstrable, must be submitted to the pragmatic test. Does it allow us to account in a satisfactory way for our experiences? Through James's realism we may find that objective reality is neither as secure, reliable, and divorced from human influence nor that the determination of values is so utterly capricious and ephemeral as we might be led to believe. The point, then, is that the search for the public good need not proceed in the manner of a search for some Absolute Good that is fixed, universal, and "out there," though both idealists and skeptics, from their contrary positions, would wish to impose this definition of the problem.

Another example of vicious abstractionism that has hindered understanding of the public interest and the public good is the concept of pluralism. Again, the concept is potentially very useful by drawing attention to the variety and diversity in social life, but the concept becomes static, uncritical, and useless when it no longer permits one to see the reality of continuities and wholes. When wholeness and continuity are perceived, at best, as only fictional or nominal, then the concept of pluralism has lost value as a working idea. And again, the approach of pragmatism is radically empirical. The exact balance of the one and the many, wholeness and plurality, continuity of experience and discontinuity, is something that must be uncovered through the experiential process of verification. The pragmatist only begins with the reflection "that conjunctions and separations are, at all events, co-ordinate phenomena which, if we take experiences at their face value, must be accounted equally real."[6] The position of pragmatism is to "equally abjure absolute monism and absolute pluralism. The world is One just so far as its parts hang together by any definite connexion. It is many just so far as any definite connexion fails to obtain."[7] If pluralism is used as a critical, empirical concept, it will not necessarily lead to automatic assumptions about the ubiquitous diversity in society, but will help highlight the contrast between real diversity and equally real conformity. What do we mean when we call a society pluralistic? Pluralism of what? Of institutions? Of voluntary associations? Of cultural patterns? Of ideologies? When the term is pinned down it can be seen that the American political system is in some ways pluralistic and in other ways not. It may not be difficult to confirm that diffusion of power, proliferation of political arenas, social and institutional checks on power, and the technical fact of many voluntary groups and associations all contribute to a certain pluralism. Beyond this there is probably just as much evidence that the United States is extraordinarily homogeneous. Some observers have been struck by the sameness, conformity, and orthodoxy of American life, the common cultural experience imposed by electronic media, the social-psychological pattern of other-direction, and the regimenting forces of technology.[8]

Yet another effect "intellectualism" has had on conventional wisdom about the public interest is to contribute to the image of the common good the character of a closed system of truth, a single value leaving no options open for the future and terminating discussion of goals in the present. An interesting product of this outlook is Thomas Landon Thorson's *The Logic of Democracy*. Thorson convincingly shows why such closed systems of thought should be avoided and proceeds to latch onto Peirce's description of his basic rule of reason, "Do not block the way of inquiry," a statement from what Thorson praises as "perhaps as profound a paragraph as has ever been written."[9] Thorson takes this caveat and translates it into a fundamental philosophical recommendation on behalf of political democracy: "Do not block the possibility of change with respect to social goals."[10] Though Thorson may be on the right track in reacting against closed systems, he falls into an abstractionist trap by misinterpreting the unique position of Peirce and the pragmatists. He contends that "the principle of fallibilism does not say that we can never know the truth, but rather that we are never justified in behaving as if we knew it";[11] but, as was shown for Peirce, and James as well, we are always acting "as if" and it is perfectly sensible to act on such a basis because only through such activity is it possible to verify the truth of all those things we supposed, hypothesized, or "knew about." In place of a stilted, absolutist, closure Thorson has put a stilted, abstract openness, whereas the pragmatist is merely trying to point out that "openness" and "closure" are invariably mixed together in the world and in our own experience of knowing and acting. Life is what we make of it, but in making anything of it life is an endless series of closures, of options shut off and roads not taken. In the configuration of belief and doubt various issues are thrown open, but empirically there are also beliefs that we are perfectly willing to act on, and that we must act on, even though they may be as fallible as the beliefs put under examination. Exactly what absolute openness in inquiry and action would look like empirically is rather difficult to imagine. Therefore, when Thorson recommends that there should always be the possibility of change with respect to social goals, included in the very recommendation itself is the assumption that there are social goals. These goals are not absolute—for that would nullify his original recommendation[12]—yet they are presumably the guide to particular actions that represent real closures. What else can be said but that the public is acting "as if" these goals are the best? But do these goals block the way of change? Thorson's recommendation may be helpful if taken in a pragmatic sense as a guide to action that admits the empirical mix of openness and closure in the context of human action; the determination of social goals is not an all or nothing proposition but a search for partial closures that work. In the form of "vicious abstractionism," the commitment to an "open" society becomes a rationale for immobility or the basis for neglecting questions of the public good. This can be avoided only by appreciating that the public interest can be made intelligible without fear of commitment to some closed system of truth.

The tentative conceptualization of the public good given above thus serves to clear away useless stumbling blocks to inquiry. It declares no need to prove some whole and complete Public Good any more than science need, or even can, *prove* some whole and complete Objective Reality; inquiry into the public good is no more or less mysterious than examining any other issue of human beliefs and values. This conceptualization also assumes that the connections and wholeness of social life are as subject to empirical investigation as is the disconnectedness and plurality of social life. What needs to be shown is how pragmatism recasts the problem of the public good in realistic, empirical terms.

Though larger philosophical issues are not necessarily resolved through our tentative formulation of the public interest as the result of the pragmatic process of verification, it is possible to examine the various analytical roles that the concept may play in political inquiry. The germ of this analysis, its starting point, is not the larger speculative question of the absolutist; rather, it is nothing more baffling or inscrutable than the continual struggle to find the most successful way of coping with the affairs of the public. The problem of determining the public good takes on a concrete, experiential, and intelligible character when the first recognition in our experience of *public* objects of attention, as something subject to human inquiry, action, manipulation, and creation sets in motion the intricate and incessant processes of verifying our beliefs about such objects. In accounting for the status of the public interest, therefore, the most obvious task of political analysis is to identify the existence and scope of public problems; as Dewey explains, "The outstanding problem of the Public is discovery and identification of itself."[13] Dewey contends that traditional liberal analysis has made a full discovery and appreciation of the public very difficult. The public may be hidden by reducing all problems to their relation to private interest groups, which is simply an extension of the liberal tendency to put social problems in individual terms. Though appearing politically realistic, this analysis manifests a tension between material culture, which "is verging upon the collective and corporate," and our moral culture, which, "along with our ideology, is, on the other hand, still saturated with ideals and values of an individualism derived from the prescientific, pretechnological age."[14] The result often is that explanation of and responsibility for the public condition are stripped of any political features. The best reflection of this is the ambivalence over technology and modern organization that represents a collective experience in American society. On the one hand, their potential value for man is impressive; they hold out the possibility of new products and services that make life easier, and the possibility for efficient distribution of these goods. Yet every advance seems to have its destructive by-product: new communications mean a threat to privacy, large institutions a threat to personal identity, automobiles mean tearing up neighborhoods for new roads, various sources of power lead to more and more pollution. What is interesting is how often this ambivalence leads to the questioning of science and technology and a romanticism about a simpler life. Do we really want the technological benefits, if these are the consequences? But the fact of a technological and bureaucratized society represents the accumulated and diffuse consequences of many particular discoveries and events; it represents our identity as a public, that is, the kind of public we are. In this sense, the various problems that were mentioned only partially result from technology; they also result from human decisions and goals regarding the use of technology or, more to the point, from the lack of coordination of goals in relation to those decisions. It is not at all clear, for example, that ecological deterioration (or at least forms of it) are really problematic in technological terms. Science and technology are only superficially the villain; yet it is curious how human frustration, sufficiently sensitive to the backlash created by human inventions, does not more often lead people to the conclusion that there is some fundamental weakness in their conception of political organization. The discovery of the public is precisely the discovery of those objective conditions that, though resulting from particular individual and private group actions, have a collective effect and invite, by their very disturbing presence, collective and cooperative solutions. The discovery of the public includes not only the notion of a shared social condition but the notion that such conditions are susceptible to cooperative regulation and control on the part of the affected group—the public organized into the state.

The raw material for an analysis of the public interest is provided not only by a study of the indirect consequences of social transactions but also by the examination of the doubts that may be raised about the conventional accounts of such phenomena. A number of observations that have recently been pushed to the foreground of our political experience may stimulate an irritating doubt that no longer allows easy satisfaction with the eclipse of the public interest idea. Recent developments in America indicate an increasing concern with new kinds of social issues and with new ways of looking at old social issues. Fresh attention is being paid to the quality of life and to problems with such diffuse ramifications that they affect the plight of most, if not all, citizens. It is becoming increasingly difficult to isolate and contain social issues as private, local, and limited ills. Marshall McLuhan has identified this phenomenon:

Electric speed in bringing all social and political functions together in a sudden implosion has heightened human awareness of responsibility to an intense degree. It is this implosive factor that alters the position of the Negro, the teenager, and some other groups. They can no longer be *contained,* in the political sense of limited association. They are now involved in our lives, as we in theirs, thanks to the electric media.[15]

Problems of minority group relations, civil rights, urban decay, every variety of ecological deterioration, drug abuse, and even war have all taken on a special character. They are not socially or geographically localized in their impact; they cannot be easily evaded through social or geographic mobility. This situation has eliminated for modern man a classical alternative: escape and a new beginning, precisely the alternative that began this country. McLuhan's use of the term "implosion" vividly suggests the way in which people are becoming increasingly affected by and sensitive to the common conditions of life which they share with others, and how more and more people feel the effects of social problems even though they are some distance from the cause. For various reasons we have all become participants, willingly or not, in the diverse difficulties of a whole nation and a whole world. But whatever the cause, these developments would seem to have great significance for our political thinking and discourse. More precisely, it may be important to discuss the possibility and the desirability of cooperative, rational solutions to problems of an increasingly public character.

In *Freedom and Culture,* Dewey suggests that the salience of social interdependence may have disrupting effects on our political consciousness. "The telegraph, telephone and radio report events going on over the whole face of the globe. They are for the most part events about which the individuals who are told of them can do nothing, except to react with a passing emotional excitation,"[16] a reaction that encourages the development of conformity, propaganda, and uncritical opinion. This has bearing on "what now seems to us the over-simplification of the democratic idea indulged in by the authors of our republican government."[17] The oversimplification is the idea of the localized, omni-competent citizen protecting his private interests. Through an emphasis on communications and information, Dewey points to the problem of how men deal with a new range of problems and with greater exposure to and knowledge about such problems. What he criticizes is the lack of that kind of organized, directed use of intelligence that has been put to work so vigorously in the pursuit of private gain.[18] This use of knowledge occurred, of course, because of a particular cultural climate, but the difficulties man is beginning to confront in coping with the explosion of information combined with evidence of increased social interdependence suggest that the formal and organized use of knowledge must now be mobilized for collective social direction if man is to exert the kind of control over his life that is the essence of freedom. The one point Dewey insists on is that the shape that science takes and the very structure of knowledge and information generated in a society is a pragmatic result of existing beliefs about what society needs. Liberal thought was an appropriate and effective response to the need to "emancipate individuals from restrictions imposed upon them by the inherited type of social organization," but "the beliefs and methods of earlier liberalism were ineffective when faced with the problems of social organization and integration."[19] The difficulty Dewey then points to is the lack of a satisfying relationship between the increasingly exposed problems of public life and the existing paradigms of thought: "It is the tragedy of earlier liberalism that just at the time when the problem of social organization was most urgent, liberals could bring to its solution nothing but the conception that intelligence is an individual possession."[20]

The question of the public interest crops up because the confusing and frustrating problems that seem to afflict society at large are placed up against the posture of group theory, and the result is disorienting, inconclusive, and uneasy. The question suggested by the pragmatic line of analysis is whether or not the apathy, frustration, cynicism, etc., which may characterize citizen attitudes toward politics constitute an expression of doubt about a politics built around private interests. Further, as McLuhan and Dewey suggest, this doubt may be heightened or taken more seriously by the greater salience of the collective, public quality of many problems. Perhaps social inquiry should be turned increasingly toward some cogent analysis and understanding of the public interest in the same way that individual and private self-interest and intelligence became such a dominant and directing theme upon the breakdown of the feudal world.

Interestingly, although there is resistance to the idea of the public good in liberal politics, the problems of the public and the need for intelligent response have elicited reactions that provide a basis for analyzing the public good. One aspect of the eclipse of the public interest in our thinking is that even where cases are found that represent an attempt to adjust analytical approaches to the realities of the public's problems, there is seldom awareness that this has anything to do with the public interest. For example, local elites in America gradually came to see that a vast number of the physical, technological, and economic problems of their cities were to a great extent the result of chaotic, undirected, and uncontrolled responses to the total "urban system" and the lack of "planning." What is curious about the now commonplace interest in systematic planning processes is that the ramifications for political processes and institutions have been so little attended to. Plans developed out of an integrated perspective on the part of experts are presented to city councils made up of the guardians of wards and special interests and to public hearings where approval is acquired, painfully or not, on some small, particular aspect of the larger mosaic. Perhaps this lack of fit between planning and political processes has caused a sense of frustration on the part of the citizen ("They decide to tell us about things after all the plans are made and can't be changed") as well as cynicism on the part of the planning experts ("The citizens are simply an irritating obstacle to surmount in putting our integrated, rational plan into action").

Curiously, given the attention to planning and policy analysis that seems to employ the kind of "integrated" outlook suggested by Dewey, the notion of a "public interest" is still put in Bentley's category of "soul stuff." But despite the empirical grounding of the public itself, the empirical identification of the "public's business," and the treating of this business as an objective for human control and regulation, the idea of the public good is still not accounted for. It has been argued that in attempting to run the affairs of the public, the determinations that are made about what is good for the public represent neither capricious, individual opinion nor an Absolute Good; but what do they represent? Real understanding of the public good will have to depend on an account of the pragmatic approach to the determination of values.

NOTES

1. William James, *The Meaning of Truth*, pp. 246–250.
2. James, Meaning, pp. 249–250.
3. William James, *Pragmatism*, pp. 160–61.
4. James, *Pragmatism*, p. 145.
5. James, *Pragmatism*, p. 59.
6. William James, *Essays in Radical Empiricism*, p. 51.
7. James, *Pragmatism*, p. 105.
8. See David Riesman, Herbert Marcuse, Hannah Arendt, *The Human Condition;* Marshall McLuhan, Alexis de Tocqueville.
9. Thomas Landon Thorson, p. 120.
10. Thorson, p. 139.
11. Thorson, p. 122.
12. Thorson claims that "No one man, no group, whether minority or majority, is ever justified in claiming a right to make decisions for the whole society on the grounds that it knows what the 'right' decisions are," p. 139.
13. John Dewey, *The Public and its Problems*, p. 185.
14. John Dewey, *Individualism: Old and New*, p. 74.
15. McLuhan, p. 20.
16. John Dewey, *Freedom and Culture*, p. 44.
17. Dewey, *Freedom*, p. 45.
18. Dewey, *Freedom*, p. 134.
19. John Dewey, *Liberalism and Social Action*, p. 28.
20. Dewey, *Liberalism*, p. 45.

CHAPTER EIGHT

PRAGMATIC VALUE JUDGMENTS

In trying to conceive of the public good as the result of a pragmatic process of verification and in trying to discover how such a formulation can be put to work, one aspect that needs closer attention is the fact that the public good involves statements of purpose and value. Because of the now conventional distinction between facts and values, it may be difficult to accept the notion that the pragmatic approach can be used to generate not only factual truths about reality but intelligible values as guides to action. Yet exactly such a notion is entailed if it is to be understood that determinations of the public good can have some rational standing, that they are neither mysteries nor matters of mere opinion. Pragmatism suggests how purposes, goals, and values can be secured as forms of belief in the same way beliefs about objective reality are secured.

In approaching the problem of values, the pragmatist attempts to find a path between rationalist assertions of an End Value and a narrow utilitarian and relativist ethics. The criticism of idealized ultimate ends has already been noted as a case in point of the attack on "vicious abstractionism." More generally, the rejection of such absolutes grows out of the pragmatic attempt to tie human reason to human experience. John Dewey records the historical separation between the practical and experimental on the one hand and the rational, intellectual, and moral on the other hand—respectively, the lower and higher realms. Both religion and philosophy deprecated the role of experience "as being connected with the lower and practical activity in contrast with the superior worth of purely rational activity."[1] Through avoiding the realm of concrete experience, the study of values took on the character of an assertion of fixed, universal principles of conduct, which were held, as Charles Peirce would put it, by the methods of tenacity and scholastic authority. One result was a sharp severance between means and ends that "mark the form in which the traditional divorce of theory and practice has expressed itself in actual life,"[2] with the consequence that there is a "cultivated diffusion of ideals and aims that are separated from the conditions which are the means of actualization."[3] These tendencies have manifested themselves in a view of ethics as the establishment of some definition of the good that is above and beyond experience and acts as a point to which we direct ourselves. Historically, this view developed moral systems that became increasingly divorced from human conduct and irrelevant to practical affairs, whereas, for Dewey,

The problem of restoring integration and cooperation between man's beliefs about the world in which he lives and his beliefs about the values and purposes that should direct his conduct is the deepest problem of modern life. It is the problem of any philosophy that is not isolated from that life.[4]

Exclaims James, "Our faculties of belief were not primarily given us to make orthodoxies and heresies withal; they were given us to live by."[5]

In determining the purposes that make up the public good, the search for some ultimate end is fruitless to the extent that such searches have been conducted without any corrective, working relation to experience, to how such ends operate to satisfy human needs. This is not to say that the content of abstract ethical systems is *prima facie* irrelevant but only that what relevance they may have can only be appreciated through the transformation of ultimate values into some kind of workable values. But if the approach of absolute end values has been inadequate, the utilitarian-relativist approach is equally unsatisfactory. This philosophical reaction was helpful in relating human values to desires and satisfactions, but it failed to respond adequately to certain serious flaws of the earlier rationalism. Dewey points out, for example, that "empirical theories retain the notion that thought and judgment are concerned with values that are experienced independently of them."[6] What is different from the absolutist position is the form that this independence takes; rather than the independence of a higher order of truth, it is the independence of subjective responses seen as pains and pleasures. Utility theory does not tend to see values as the result of an experience that is subject to human control; thus values become casual, whimsical, and static rather than a guide to creative activity. The notion of utility is such a sharp reaction to rationalism that it is able to see values only as subjective impulses. By ignoring the human element in the formation of the very objects of value, "the theory in question holds down value to objects *antecedently* enjoyed, apart from reference to the method by which they come into existence; it takes enjoyments which are casual because unregulated by intelligent operations to be values in and of themselves."[7] Ironically, a utilitarian and subjectivist view of values ends up asserting the fixity of values almost as much as absolutism does, but in this case what is fixed about values is the feeling that they are somehow "given" and already fulfilled by their very expression; they are fixed in their "bare existence." Dewey explains this point by distinguishing between terms such as "enjoyed" and "satisfying" as opposed to "enjoyable" and "satisfactory":

To say that something is enjoyed is to make a statement about a fact, something already in existence; it is not to judge the value of the fact. There is no difference between such a proposition and one which says that something is sweet or sour, red or black. . . . The fact that something is desired only raises the *question* of its desirability; it does not settle it.[8]

But the question of values gets beyond these assertions of fact, which are all that the pain/pleasure principle holds out as an ethic. The question of values enters not with the claim that something is enjoyed, desirable, or satisfying but, for example, with the assertion that something is satisfactory. Dewey explains this critical distinction:

To declare something *satisfactory* is to assert that it meets specified conditions. It is, in effect, a judgment that the thing "will do." It involves a prediction; it contemplates a future in which the thing will continue to serve; it *will* do. It asserts a consequence the thing will actively institute: it will *do*. That it is satisfying is the content of a proposition of fact; that it is satisfactory is a judgment, an estimate, an appraisal. It denotes an attitude *to be* taken, that of striving to perpetuate and to make secure.[9]

Contrary to static measures of utility, the whole idea of a value is that it serves to identify something that "ought" to be, and in so doing, if a value is to be intelligible, it directs attention to possible consequences of action, to what will or might occur. Units of pleasure are not things that *ought* to be desired; they are merely things that *are* desired.[10]

Viewed in this way, utility value results in the separation of means and ends, with the former becoming a narrow calculus of a quantitative sort and the latter becoming merely a fixed and question-begging "given." By reducing value questions to utility, a self-contained practical ethic develops in which the very context that defines practicality is left unexplored. The entrepreneurial ethic begs the political question of the value of free enterprises; the ethic of bargaining begs the political question of the value of interest-based politics; in such cases certain fundamental values are un-reflected upon, taken for granted. Thus, "there is something abnormal and in the strict sense impossible in mere means, in, that is, instruments totally dissevered from ends."[11] One result, for example, is that "the attempt to assimilate other activities to the model of economic activity (defined as a calculated pursuit of gain) reverses the state of the facts," for the pursuit of gain "is not a primary fact which can be used to account for other phenomena . . . it is subject to examination, criticism and valuation in the light of the place it occupies in the system of developing activities."[12] Though the end cannot be ignored, neither can it be adequately treated in terms of utility since the end is "out of sight," to use a favorite phrase of Josiah Royce, and the formulation of the end may be in contradiction to the "socially prevailing habit of regarding enjoyments as they are actually experienced as value in and of themselves."[13] The establishment of ends guides one beyond things "actually experienced as values" to things potentially experienced as values, which is the sense in which the principle of maximizing utility must be taken. As soon as it is taken in this sense, such maxi-mization leads to values that, on their face, seem impractical and nonuseful. But this is because they assert a more encompassing satisfactoriness that is at the moment only a possibility and that, as a guide to action, may call into question the momentary fact that existing habits actually satisfy. Thus, every immediate good is not a terminal value nor a fixed ground for identifying values but a fillip to the exploration of further possibilities.

For the pragmatist, then, both absolute value and utility value are mistaken in that they are separated from empirical-pragmatic analysis of the real world. Value considerations have moved on a whole separate track from the rest of intellectual life and the pragmatist suggests that the convergence between the two be understood. The first corrective that the pragmatist makes is to point out that the real issue concerns not facts and values, but the *true* and the *good;* after all, values are simply facts. Confusion on this point has often loaded the case against value judgments. Thus, Arnold Brecht contends that "factual research and strictly logical inferences offer possibilities of intersubjective verification that are not available in the case of ultimate value judgments."[14] What is Brecht comparing; sense data versus Absolute Values? Is that what is really at stake, are the two really comparable? When it is said that facts are intersubjectively verifiable, what can that mean but that there are truths about them that can be shared through common experience of consequences? It is truth that is shared, and in the same sense we can speak of the intersubjective verification of the *good*, for, as we found James saying, the true is an expedient for our knowing and the good is an expedient for our acting. Indeed, for James, the true is itself a form of the good; it tells us what we ought to believe. This requires that values be viewed as hypotheses that serve to regulate behavior and direct it to successful outcomes; values are thus guides to a successful art of self-regulation and self-creation. Thus, we know the good just as we know the true, on the basis of its pragmatic success.[15]

It was argued earlier that the conditions that provide the public with its identity include no ends that are given by virtue of the very existence of the public; in this context some determination of the public good must take place. Though ends are not given, by the same token the situation in which the public finds itself in relation to purposes and ends is not *tabula rasa*. The search for ends, like the search for a philosophical starting point, is not abstract but rather begins with the state of mind in which you actually find yourself. Actual doubt about values means that doubt about what is desired is not thoroughgoing, just as doubts about objective reality are also not comprehensive. As many operative beliefs about reality are not under question, so also many objects of value are accepted. That these objects are desired is, as Dewey points out, simply a fact. Thus, the quest for some end to action is stimulated in the same manner as the quest for truth; that is, the pattern of values is problematic in the same way that the juxtaposition of events in our experience is problematic. Discontinuities, tensions, unpredictabilities urge one to find more satisfying and effective truths about reality; by the same token, stirrings of doubt lead to the rejection of the notion that actual desired objects represent the limit of the good. These values are doubted because they do not work; they contradict each other; their immediate attraction leads to distasteful consequences; they compete for control over our attention. To this extent they do not do what they are supposed to do, that is, act as a satisfactory guide to human judgment and action, and so doubt stimulates the search for some view of the good that will help order desires into some workable and productive plan—in concrete terms, this is what the "search for the good" entails.

What pragmatism proposes, therefore, is the establishment of what Dewey calls an "end-in-view," which is not a fixed end but a tentative working principle. To say that it is good "consists in the meaning that is experienced to belong to an activity when conflict and entanglement of various compatible impulses and habits terminate in a unified and orderly release in action."[16] The good, to put it simply, can be experienced, which suggests that a thing which we envision or idealize as good "becomes an aim or end only when it is worked out in terms of concrete conditions available for its realization, that is, in terms of its 'means.' "[17] By virtue of its experimental character, the end-in-view is constantly subject to reformulation and clarification; moral life grows and evolves by literally being lived. The end is thus no longer like a limit to be reached but like the operative principle of an intelligible process of transforming the world. Since the end works in this way, it is possible to say that "in a strict sense an end-in-view is a *means* in present action."[18]

But how and why do we come by these ends-in-view? You can come by them any way you want. Pragmatism only sets up the conditions for making them intelligible human ends. As for the question "why?"—James answers, in accord with Dewey's view, that such ends are set up so as to help "satisfy at all times as many demands as we can."[19] These ends are the result of one "unconditional commandment, which is that we should seek incessantly, with fear and trembling, so to vote and to act as to bring about the very largest total universe of good which we can see."[20] On its face, this rationale for setting up ends-in-view seems to be a reversion to the utilitarian rule of maximizing pleasure, and indeed this is at least partially the case. The difference is that the pragmatist throws open the doors to the full range of human demands above and beyond, and perhaps even qualitatively distinct from, the existing patterns of habitual enjoyments. Though pragmatism is an adjustment of certain utilitarian themes, it is equally, though less obviously, an attempt to bring "ultimate" ends into the practical context of their realization. James is not trying to oppose ideals with mundane needs for satisfaction but, along with Dewey, he is trying to show what is required to make religious and ethical ideals workable principles, how the good is to be not merely reverenced but experienced. Where the utilitarian might say that what *does* work is good, the pragmatist asserts that what is really good *will* work. Though the terminology may be misleading, pragmatism leaves a wide berth for the operation of ideals. It only attacks ideals seen as a deprecation of human experience, as ultimate limits that do not speak to the concrete problems of action or contribute to an art of living. Thus, pragmatism is as much an attempt to concretize and actualize the visions of the absolutist as it is an attempt to ennoble the impulses of the utilitarian. Since it is impossible to know in advance some complete good, it is necessary to use experience as the guide to the "richer universe,"

the good which seems most organizable, most fit to enter into complex combinations, most apt to be a member of a more inclusive whole. But which particular universe this is he (the philosopher) cannot know for certain in advance; he only knows that if he makes a bad mistake the cries of the wounded will soon inform him of the fact.[21]

The good is set up as an end-in-view and, by virtue of being tentative and not *a priori*, it is "held only as a working hypothesis until results confirm its rightness."[22] Therefore, mistakes

are lessons in wrong methods of using intelligence and instructions as to a better course in the future. They are indications of the need of revision, development, readjustment. Ends grow, standards of judgment are improved. . . . Moral life is protected from falling into formalism and rigid repetition.[23]

How do we come to see the end-in-view as a good in the first place and how do we continue to experience it as a good? The answer to the first question is very similar to the way in which beliefs develop as assertions of what is true: they appeal somehow to imagination; they develop as plausible hypotheses. The exact source is immaterial; the point is that belief in a good strikes one as a directive worth following, suggests itself as the possible resolution of doubt about the existing objects of value, and collects wants and desires in the most coherent unity. The process of experiencing the good then requires that the end-in-view be analyzed and framed in terms of the conditions for its realization such that it can inform us, in the practical context, not merely about what is desired but about what ought to be desired, that is, what is desirable. The end reveals itself as a good insofar as the effects of the actions it directs constitute an ever-increasing satisfaction of more and more inclusive and coherent desires. The contradiction between seemingly inconsistent and opposite goods, the constant tension between many present objects of desire, is what has to be worked out. Since the practical problem is usually a problem of goods that are both competing and incommensurable, a method is needed for sorting out the *best whole* of goods. This cannot be done by a quantitative calculus but only by intelligent deliberation and making hard choices to determine what actions will have the *kind* of consequences that will satisfy the most demands. "There is hardly a good," says James, "which we can imagine except as competing for the possession of the same bit of space and time with some other imagined good;" for this reason "the ethical philosopher's demand for the right scale of subordination in ideals is the fruit of an altogether practical need."[24] What determines this scale of subordination? The answer requires some measure of the consequences to be expected, specifically of whether those consequences effectively overcome tensions and inconsistencies.

Though pragmatism offers an intelligible approach to the synthesizing of partial and limited values, the relativist will suspect that at some point, at some terminus to this pragmatic development of ethics, we must necessarily be thrown back into incommensurable plurality and diversity. This might be compared to a similar issue in regard to the question of truth. Why not accept the world as an atomistic, chaotic sand-heap of events? The pragmatist's answer was that in examining the world empirically, in an attempt to resolve doubts, it is discovered that the chaos of events is only partial; not only are there discontinuities but there are also continuities. Connections in our experiences are found to make sense and, by affecting our activity, to work out successfully. What radical empiricism discloses is not the plurality of the world, but the mixture of plurality and unity. The question about the relativity of values is answered along much the same lines. The multitude of affective preferences are not the sum and finality of empirical explanations; experience points not only to the multiplicity of values and disagreement over them, but also to conformity and agreement over values. Moreover, it discloses that such agreement may be to a great extent the result of human deliberation and action. Millions of people spread around the world assert a common commitment to the value of a particular set of religious doctrines. Millions of Americans commonly consent to the worth of constitutional processes by accepting without threat of violence the results of national elections, which should be an impressive display of shared commitment to the value of a process. Even the historian Daniel Boorstin, who makes so much of the American rejection of social blueprints, admits that "we have at the same time an overweening sense of orthodoxy."[25]

The relativist may counter with the claim that, despite the obvious conformity that may be observed about what is considered good, there is still no intelligible, reliable means of exchanging values in the way that facts are exchanged. Facts are submitted to methods of proof, but when it comes to values, we live by our impulses and our wits and if many people come to the same conclusion, that is a result of fortune or convenience, not rational deliberation. Epistemologically, statements about what is and statements about what ought to be have a completely different standing. But this distinction is highly overdrawn and problematic. How does one share his beliefs about reality except by encouraging someone to share his subjective situation? What he implicitly says is, "If you don't believe what I'm saying, put yourself in my position, see the world as I'm seeing it, do what I've done, perform this experiment and you will come out with the same consequences. What I expect to happen, you will discover." Facts do not speak the same way to everyone because each person's consciousness, each field of attention, may not be the same. What makes possible a shared understanding is not some fixed relation of idea and object but the function of the idea as a plan of action, that is, as a possible experiment that can be performed by different people. Truth appears as both relative and objective, relative in that it depends on the context in which it is understood, but objective in that it relates to activities that are carried out with concrete results in the world.[26] The promotion of a particular value takes place through a test in which one person challenges another to share his perspective to see if it works. The challenge might go something like this: "On the face of it you and I seem to disagree about what is good in this situation, but I am convinced that if we frame goals in these terms, they will serve to fulfill the good I claim for them in addition to fulfilling your good better than you expected. One of us, in any case, may be misled about the value of his goals and if all of the consequences of our respective positions are examined we may find a point of convergence. But the only way of telling this is to see what works, to conjointly experiment with our values the same way we can conjointly experiment about truth." If the good is that which resolves the greatest tensions and contradictions, then surely its subjectiveness is balanced off by the objective consequences that provide a measure of its success. The entrepreneur seeking profits may assert the value of free enterprise as the best end-in-view; though his position may seem subjective, the application of this value generates a rigorous test of it. Principles of free enterprise may end up leading to actual monopolization and cyclical economic depressions; and such consequences represent the objectification of the particular end-in-view, which may suggest the reformulation and amendment of such ends to include values that were earlier considered incommensurable with the pursuit of profit.

It is also said that it is impossible to derive an "ought" statement from an "is" statement; as a matter of logic, that may technically be correct. Yet, in pragmatic terms, the consequence of our knowledge of reality for our values is obviously very great; indeed, many conflicts over social issues, though they are of an ethical character, can be greatly clarified and resolved if certain questions about man and society can be answered. For example, regarding the treatment of criminals, ought they to be punished or rehabilitated? One side of the argument may advance some value of retribution and the other side's position may involve some humanitarian value to changing the criminals' behavior. Yet, aside from either of these considerations, there may be a shared value in ridding the society of crime and this issue may turn on the empirical question of whether one or the other method of dealing with criminals *is* more effective in meeting this end. Further, discovery of the most effective way to rid the society of crime may lead to the inclusion of some satisfaction of those value claims over which the disputants seemed to disagree originally. The points of contact in the concrete experiences and normative claims of people provide the groundwork for a prescriptive analysis of the differences among their larger structure of values. In the particular context of such analysis, empirical knowledge of what "is" does resolve *de facto* certain questions about what "ought" to be, and this occurs because differences over values are not total, because there are continuities as well as discontinuities in the ethical life of a society.

The dependence that is experienced between the true and the good also goes the other way; not only can ethical problems actually be resolved through an examination of consequences, but also a fully experimental method in trying to understand the world is actually dependent on certain values. This, it will be recalled, is the "will to believe" argument of James. It works by simply reversing the above examples: in order really to know how to treat criminals, it will be necessary to make a commitment to one approach over the other—that is, to set up rehabilitation, for example, as a hypothesis. The notion that one solution should be set up as a hypothesis over the other, as opposed to doing nothing, requires, considering the lack of convincing evidence at the beginning, some unproved assertion of value. The hypothesis that criminals can be rehabilitated contains not only the suggestion that it will work, but the assertion that it would be good or better if it does work. In other words, experimentation involves activity, which involves purposes, which involve a goal or end; if we were thoroughly indifferent to crime and criminals we might never consider trying the rehabilitative or any other solution.

Though the fact/value distinction may have some logical or metaphysical standing, human experience reveals the *de facto* concrete connection between beliefs about what is good and what is true. Knowledge of the consequences of action really does help to distinguish intelligently between what is desirable and what is merely desired, as Dewey would put it; and value judgments really do act as a guide in the attempt to get at the fullest knowledge of the world.[27] In the final analysis, what makes values intelligible is the same factor that makes truth intelligible—the simple, almost tautological fact that both are products of human thought in its relation to problems of human experience. In speaking of the terms "good" and "bad," James explains:

They mean no absolute natures, independent of personal support. They are objects of feeling and desire, which have no foothold or anchorage in Being, apart from the existence of actually living minds.

Wherever such minds exist, with judgment of good and ill, and demands upon one another, there is an ethical world in its essential features.[28]

Both the good and the true are products of human fabrication resulting from man's dealings with the world, rather than attributes of external reality. In this sense, the "good" is neither a fixed ideal nor a fixed configuration of impulses, but rather the result of deliberation, testing and conjoint experience among men. It is interesting to note the similarities in the way the true and the good are actually dealt with the ethical products of this process are all around us. The ethical structure of society can be built up through situational, prescriptive analysis of the consequences of action, the forming and shaping of effective and desirable responses to human problems. Even aside from a prescriptive style of analysis (A is good because it leads to consequence X), man's social history discloses ethical growth and movement by the mere fact of the promotion of new goals not accepted in any rigorous prescriptive way, but because they recommend themselves as some larger "best whole" of human demands.

Even though ethical deliberation and prescriptive analysis of the efficacy and long-term value of goals may go a long way in clarifying normative disputes, this does not seem to answer the whole problem raised by the relativist. Much of the discussion so far seems to deal with conditional, instrumental values, but even if 99 percent of our ethical confusions and differences could be resolved by such intelligent deliberation, does not this whole ethical structure always reduce itself to some fundamental good that is not subject to such rational calculation? Is this not the point where the running analogy with truth-seeking breaks down? If every conditional value ends in a question "but why?" what is the end of the chain? What makes one think that things can be put together into some "best whole," and does not the intelligibility of the whole process rest on that assumption? The pragmatist's answer to whether there is some intelligible terminus to the chain of ethical reasoning is that he does not know, any more than he knows whether or not his "factual" explanations of the world could ever culminate in some totally adequate view of things. Thus, ends-in-view are like the scientific theories about the physical universe: they are assumed because they seem to work, they are satisfactory. The status of the belief in a unified good as the end of action is that, relative to the alternatives, it holds out the possibility of intelligent human control over the conditions of life; it is an assumption worth making because of the payoffs, because—to revert to Jame's terms—we are more interested in searching out the truth than merely avoiding error, i.e., because with ethics, just as with science, we are willing to take the risks.

The essence of this position is not that ethics is fully intelligible but that it is no less intelligible, less objective, or less revelant to human thought than our explanations of the world and the assumptions upon which they rest. In the final analysis, the criticism of the relativist emphasis on the is/ought distinction is typically pragmatic: what is the consequence of the distinction? The pragmatist wants to know how the distinction should affect our action. Does the making of the distinction cause our explanations to be any more reliable or our systems any less useful? What are we supposed to do with the distinction? Abandon the most rudimentary applications of intelligence to questions of purpose and wallow in subjectivity? Are scientific theories then also to be abandoned as mere human constructs that cannot be proven? The essential weakness of the conventional distinction between "is" and "ought" is that belief in it does not seem to contribute any relevant or significant guidance to the problem of knowing how the world works or how to work better in the world.

The abstract and irrelevant character of the relativist's distinction becomes clear when it is put in the context of human experience and human problems. Why should we believe that our subjective impulses in relation to pains and pleasures represent the limit of the ethical universe? Are not some pains and pleasures of our own making? If so, why do we not make whole new pleasures, higher pleasures? The problem is that the feeling that the is/ought distinction is somehow consequential has infected social thought, and the result has not only been the rejection of certain social goods requiring cooperative effort as rationally untenable, but also the instigation of larger "pains" that people create and then suffer and try to escape because of the default of effective human control. Urban crowding and waste, pollution, depletion of natural resources, wage-price spirals, and, in general, limits on the creative and free use of human potential have resulted, to a certain extent, from a kind of social thinking having as one of its main features an unpragmatic, abstract commitment to value relativism. Historically, the notion of scientific value relativism may have performed a valuable function as part of the larger struggle to unleash human thought from traditional bonds, and in this sense many of its effects have surely been progressive. But liberal relativism imposes a value that simply may not work very well any more—the prescription that we ought to avoid the attempt to formulate substantive public goals because the only secure goods we can identify are the multitude of purely individual wants.

Explaining the world and deciding how to change it are problems that are not in completely separate orbits, but are jointly grounded in human experience. Knowledge of the true and the good are intermixed in human action. When we appreciate this pragmatic perspective on values, we begin to understand what kind of problem we are talking about when we speak of determining the public good. We are talking about public problem-solving and action in pursuit of a viable end-in-view, and the testing of the satisfactoriness of such an end through the consequences it generates. The essential problem of public agreement on public ends brings the general problem of values into the realm of political action, and the problem of the public good must now be pursued in that context.

NOTES

1. John Dewey, *On Experience, Nature and Freedom,* p. 76.
2. Dewey, *The Quest for Certainty,* p. 280.
3. Dewey, *Quest,* p. 282.
4. Dewey, *Quest,* p. 255.
5. William James, *The Will to Believe,* p. 56.
6. Dewey, *Quest,* p. 257.
7. Dewey, *Quest,* p. 258.
8. Dewey, *Quest,* p. 260.
9. Dewey, *Quest,* pp. 260–261.
10. Dewey, *Experience, and Nature,* pp. 396–397.
11. Dewey, *Human Nature and Conduct,* p. 219.
12. Dewey, *Human Nature,* p. 220.
13. Dewey, *Quest,* p. 259.
14. Arnold Brecht, pp. 298–299.
15. Josiah Royce sees this connection operating at the very root of our cognitive processes: ". . . the objective world is not known as prior to the cognitive responses, but is viewed as it is because the conscious process regards itself as meaning a reponse to a situation . . . I acknowledge a particular fact, then, in connection with a particular attempt at action." Royce, *The World and the Individual,* Vol. II, p. 31.

16. Dewey, *Human Nature*, p. 210.
17. Dewey, *Human Nature*, p. 234.
18. Dewey, *Human Nature*, p. 226.
19. James, p. 205.
20. James, p. 209.
21. James, p. 210.
22. Dewey, *Reconstruction in Philosophy*, p. 175.
23. Dewey, *Reconstruction*, p. 175.
24. James, pp. 202–203,
25. Daniel Boorstin, pp. 13–14.
26. Sidney Hook, p. 157.
27. For two books which develop this point in the context of the physical sciences, see Thomas S. Kuhn and Stephen Toulmin.
28. James, p. 197.

CHAPTER NINE

THE METHOD OF AUTHORITY

The examination of the pragmatic approach to the formation of beliefs was undertaken because the public interest partakes of the broader issues of truth and values as human beliefs and because any political philosophy must establish some standpoint on these general considerations. To know what the public good is one must know what he means by the good in general, yet that much having been settled, one must then look to the special features of the public good. What unique kind of belief is this? In what context does it operate? What special problems are raised, and is our approach to beliefs in general appropriate to these problems?

The first unique feature of the public good is that it refers to beliefs that are social, which means that the "determination of the public good" refers not merely to the settlement of belief on the part of an individual but to arriving at an agreement among several people. The pragmatic process of verification will have to be conjointly experienced and this may develop on the basis of the root fact that one thing men experience in their attempt to formulate accounts of the world is the consequences of other men's actions. Practice becomes the concrete, inter-subjective link in human knowledge.[1] The second unique feature of the public good is that it is even a special form of social belief, that is, belief set within the peculiar context of the public's dilemma. This dilemma was earlier identified by the dual circumstance under which the public operates: the need to act, to grasp control of the public's problems, and to submit them to human mastery combined with the congenital lack of goals and continual uncertainty of what common purposes there should be.

Though it is important to place the issue of the public good within the context of the public's dilemma, the fact is that the realities of this dilemma are sufficiently distressing that a great deal of the discussion of the public good through history has been inclined to deny, ignore, or circumvent in some way the exigencies of this dual circumstance. Idealism and determinism try to convince man that the uncertainty and openness he feels about public ends are merely the result of being blinded by ignorance of objective goals. There are objective ends and those intelligent enough to know them should tell society, should be followed by society, or perhaps impose these ends on society. On the other hand, skeptics who view all claims to the common good as capricious and subjective are willing to allow that society ought to pass up any notion of collective, conscious direction of the pressing affairs of the public based on some notion of the public good. In these cases the denial of the concrete circumstances of public life, of the dimensions of the public dilemma, leads to the promotion of views of knowledge and truth that hardly speak in a relevant way to political man. Dewey suggests that this has occurred because accounts of knowledge and discussion of political values have historically been dominated by the professional truth-seekers—philosophers and scientists—and their very special task, the "quest for certainty." It is not simply truth that they are after, the whole truth or all the truth, but the most certain truth; they are concerned with identifying the solid ground of secure and firm knowledge. Though this is a perfectly legitimate task, it is a limited one; and truth is not the exclusive concern of the professional philosopher any more than health is the exclusive concern of the physician. In recognizing this fact, pragmatism makes a vital contribution to political inquiry. It suggests a thoroughgoing pluralistic view of truth itself; it is many things to many men in many different situations, and certitude is but one virtue it may possess. Not only do we want to be certain about knowledge but we also want knowledge to work for us and do things. What the pragmatist directs our attention to is the phenomenon of belief, truth in the realm of action. The classical tradition, Dewey explains, presumes that "the certain and knowledge are co-extensive," and to this he critically replies:

In contrast with this identification, the very word "belief" is eloquent on the topic of certainty. We *believe* in the absence of knowledge or complete assurance. Hence the quest for certainty has always been an effort to transcend belief. Now since, as we have already noted, all matters of practical action involve an element of uncertainty, we can ascend from belief to knowledge only by isolating the latter from practical doing and making.[2]

Inquiry does not involve a thorough divorce from action, even though it apparently has been in the interest of the truth-seeker to see things in this way:

They all hold that the operation of inquiry excludes any element of practical activity that enters into the construction of the object known. Strangely enough this is as true of idealism as of realism, of theories of synthetic activity as of those of passive receptivity. For according to them "mind" constructs the known object not in any observable way, or by means of practical overt acts having a temporal quality, but by some occult internal operation.[3]

The "quest for certainty," having dominated our understanding of truth in the realm of politics, has bred two kinds of reactions: transcendence and withdrawal. The first is exemplified by the Platonic-Hegelian attempt to seek eternal principles, which transcend the tumult of politics but which are claimed to be appropriate to the reshaping of politics. As Hannah Arendt explains:

Still, the philosopher's rule had to be justified, and it could be justified only if the philosopher's truth possessed a validity for that very realm of human affairs which the philosopher had to turn away from in order to perceive it . . . the rule of the philosopher-king . . . is the domination of human affairs by something outside its own realm.[4]

The withdrawal reaction is represented by liberal thought with its confidence in the capacity to delimit political affairs by legal-institutional mechanisms, and its emphasis on voluntarism and individualism, which sustains the myth of an effective "escape from politics" through retreat into the realm of the purely personal where intelligence roams free and secure. Neither reaction effectively addresses the public interest because neither operates on the basis of respect for the terrain of politics, which concretely identifies the context of those beliefs that are in question when we speak of the public good.

An important contribution of pragmatism to political theory is that it offers a view of truth that is relevant to the special problems of human belief set in the context of the public's dilemma. It views truth-seeking as a matter of settling beliefs, it sees this settlement ultimately occurring through concrete experience of the consequences of action, and it is relativistic in its assessment of the value that truth may have such that it is at least as interested in the relevance, usefulness, expediency, and scope of beliefs as it is in their absolute certitude. Pragmatism therefore represents a view of truth appropriate to those kinds of beliefs that make up the public good and allows one to account for political beliefs or what might be called *political truth.*

To clarify the unique context in which the issue of public good is set, let us refashion the original question: "What is the public good?" The question itself is a bit misleading in that it suggests the need for a wholesale, seamless answer. But one would not want to interpret the issue that way any more than a scientist would want to say that the question before him is, "What is the physical universe?" The scientist, of course, is in the business of contributing to man's knowledge of that universe and of trying to articulate theories that give men a certain fix on what that universe is all about, and in this sense political man deals with the public good. The real problem is the determination, in the most rational way, of ends that are useful for guiding the public's activities. This is the real significance of the question, though it may be hoped or expected that the historical progress of such determinations will contribute to knowledge of an ever more encompassing public good.

It would also help to comment at this point on the earlier distinction between theoretical ideas and ideas-in-use. It is appropriate to expect that at both levels our ideas about the public good conform to the considerations discussed above. By virtue of the critical function of theory, it can be said that these two levels of thought are interdependent; what distinguishes them are the respective concerns to which they address themselves: 1) the theoretical issue concerns the use of the public interest concept as a critical, exploratory idea for examining the appropriateness of claims to the public interest, the fit between the condition of public affairs and the pattern of popular consciousness about these affairs, the possible directions for fruitful pursuit of the public good, and, most important of all, the critical and analytical uses of the concept for examining the consequences for political institutions, processes, and behavior of the public good as a concrete problem of political action and decision, and 2) as a practical idea-in-use the issue, in the simplest and most general sense, is how the public good is being or can be determined, accepted, and used in the formation of responses to public problems and thereby effect a satisfactory control over the indirect consequences of social life. After so much questioning about what the public good is, the discussion has arrived at a rather frustrating intersection. By virtue of the very approach that has been adopted, theory, by itself, cannot offer a definition of what the substantial public good of a society is beyond hypothetical assertions. The full verification process draws theory and practice together, and though theoretical hypotheses may be well grounded, intelligently formulated, and testable, anything that resembles a completed demonstration that this or that policy end is in the public interest—or more in the public interest than some alternative—must depend on the intervention of political action itself. Though theory may not be final and conclusive, though it may not fulfill the desire of the aloof philosopher for secure knowledge of ends outside the world of action, its function vis-à-vis the world of action is significant, relevant, and intensely critical. It may explore freely and widely the dimensions of possible public response and the effectiveness of the political world as it is organized in doing the job of determining the public good or interfering with it, and in the conflict between theory and practice it will consider equally whether theory or the world itself will have to be changed.

Given the way that the problem of determining the public good has been framed—settling social beliefs within the context of the dual circumstances confronting the public—the most pressing issue concerns the form and shape of the verification process through which such beliefs are settled upon. How can the public come to any determination about what is to be done? And even if and when it does, how can it know that such determinations are justifiable, that they truly represent the good of the public? What sort of process will it employ, how will it act to achieve such determination? The pragmatic approach instructs that these public beliefs must follow somewhat the pattern of an experiment. There must be some test of whether they truly consist of what the public wants, of the "best whole" of good the public is capable of discovering. It suggests that, in practice, these beliefs will display a continuing satisfactoriness, that experience will be the guide. Though the experimental model may seem plausible enough, where does the original hypothesis come from, how does a society decide to try anything, what is the peculiar cement that shapes public agreements in the first place and puts them on some sort of working basis? How can we imagine the dynamics of such public agreement occurring within the framework of the conditions that have been laid down: 1) that the agreements be pragmatically formulated to include an experimental test of their workability; and 2) that the mode of agreement be practical and realistic in light of the public dilemma of the need to act and the congenital indeterminateness of public purposes?

In considering ways in which the public might establish agreed-upon directions and goals, one method that has been taken seriously at times is spontaneity, in which people think and act together through some discovery of their common agreement. One variety of spontaneity is the interpretation of Marxism that would have historical change wait on the natural development of proletarian consciousness growing out of material developments.[5] Liberal variants of this theme are related to individualism and voluntarism. Friedrich Hayek, for example, eliminating the possibility of any complete ethical code for public guidance, falls back on the primacy of the individual's system of ends and thereby limits social ends to "the instances where individual views coincide," such ends being "merely identical ends of many individuals."[6] Hayek does not suggest an examination of the processes affecting such agreements; he is simply willing to allow the coincidence. In the romantic/democratic tradition, an interest in spontaneity sometimes appears where social agreement is imagined to be like the communal intuition of a Quaker meeting. At times, Jean-Jacques Rousseau seems to depend on this approach, as when he explains that

he who actually voices the proposal does but put into words what all have felt, and neither intrigue nor eloquence are needed to ensure the passing into law of what each has already determined to do so soon as he can be assured that his fellows will follow suit.[7]

The discovery of shared points of view and shared values is certainly a common and vital social fact, yet it is a mode of agreement too coincidental and passive to provide a positive basis for confronting the exigencies of public problems. What does one do if spontaneity does not arise? How can the public be sure of such spontaneous convergence when it is needed? It is not sufficient to depend on the spontaneous identification of public ends, for such ends, since they are not the product of conscious control and manipulation—not the product or creation of human action—may be ephemeral, unreliable, and unmanageable. Reliance on such a mode of agreement fails to reflect a realistic concern for public problems and their consequences and the need for responsive public action.

In the modern age, a most appealing approach to the problem of achieving public agreement over ends has taken the form of dedication to the power of human intelligence, specifically in the form of rational science. Though the rationalist argument takes many forms, such as Condorcet's idea of historical progress, Bentham's utilitarian calculus of pains and pleasures, Comte's social positivism, the common theme is always that the discord and indirection of society can be resolved through submission to rational ends determined through demonstrable proof—the promise of empiricism and science.[8] In the most general sense, the idea that social ends can be set and agreed upon through intelligent, empirical demonstration and proof would seem to encompass the position staked out by the pragmatists. Yet, as mentioned earlier, the views of "rationality" and "proof" contained in so many optimistic assessments of the political efficacy of human intelligence are views dominated more by the "quest for certainty" than the quest for a usable notion of the public good. This Enlightenment spirit of secular intelligence encouraged fascination with the idea that the revolution in knowledge of the physical world could be duplicated for the social world, with the result that the deliberations of political man could proceed like the deliberations of a scientific society. What stands in the way of social harmony is the lack of a sufficient display of intelligence and dispassionate reason guiding public affairs. The notion that political men can be made to agree through rational proof not only runs against the plurality of truth and the doubtfulness about any sort of certitude, but, from a pragmatic point of view, it mistakenly suggests a form of agreement in which rational decisions are separate from and prior to action itself. The experimental outlook of pragmatism blends theory and practice in the determination of ends, such that the issue is not how rationally to prove ends as a basis for action but how to determine practical hypotheses as a basis for the test of action itself. It is impractical to think that conflicts over public policy can be settled by appeals to scientific intelligence. This arrant faith in science seems directed more toward the salvation of politics from its original sin than the proper management of political business. It is an approach that may positively resist telling political man what to do while he is on the road to those elusive social ends, and the frustrations created by the actual day-to-day failure to demonstrate effectively a social end that can be "proved" may contribute as much as anything to a thoroughgoing skepticism about the public interest.

Beyond commitments to spontaneity or rational proof, a third mode of developing conjoint action in pursuit of the public good is coercion. Indeed, in one form or another, this may be the most common approach of all; where action has to be taken and people persistently disagree about what action to take, the instruments of coercion become appealing means for the imposition of orderly public response. A clarification of terms in this area is offered by Robert Dahl, who suggests that the general term "influence" be used to identify cases in which *A* influences *B* to the extent that he gets *B* to do something that *B* would not otherwise do.[9] Power, according to this usage, would indicate coercive influence in which *B*'s action is "based on the threat or expectation of extremely severe penalties or great losses."[10] Perhaps the most continuous historical association that politics has had in the history of human thought is with the idea of power and physical coercion. This association ranges all the way from Thrasymachus' "might makes right" to the intricate web of power relations in the pluralist's political marketplace. Though liberalism rejects the kind of unrestrained and deadly use of force that has characterized so much of man's political history in the form of riot, rebellion, assassination, terror, and genocide, and though liberalism sharply tempers and more evenly spreads out the pains and penalties, liberal ideology at its roots commits itself not to the elimination of power but to the effective and safe coordination of it. This is captured in the notion that the public good in liberalism at best consists of the equilibrium among groups at any given moment or the vector-sum of group forces and pressures.

The important aspect of power is not the intensity of actual or threatened penalties, but the fact that power, using Dahl's terms, only makes reference to what *B* ends up doing irrespective of the consequences of the relationship for B's attitudes, opinions, values, state of mind, or future propensities to act. For this reason, agreements that result from power relations are always limited agreements. The affected person may not really want to do what he is doing or may not know whether he wants to do what he is doing, and this ambiguity can make power relations very tenuous. This is especially clear in the most drastic examples of the use of power, where the instruments of power are physical coercion and violence; in such cases force must be continually sustained and the "agreement" becomes cursory, almost sardonically metaphorical, as if it were said that the prisoners and the guards "agree" that the prisoners will stay in prison. Agreement here is used in the loosest sense to mean that there is a common result. On a continuous, day-to-day basis, power is seldom so unvarnished and its instruments need not be physical but psychological; but whatever form power takes, it is distinguished by having to be nothing more than a one-way relationship in which the only question concerns the resources of the powerful and the effects of the use of power; the person over whom power is wielded becomes nothing more than a kind of instrument, a vehicle, a means to the end for which the power is applied.

Ironically, some of the best observations about the limitations on power come from Niccolo Machiavelli, whose reputation is that of a power theorist. What is curious is Machiavelli's commitment to the instruments of force combined with his dislike of mere power, which causes him to argue that "it is necessary for a prince to possess the friendship of the people; otherwise he has no resource in times of adversity."[11] To the notion that the accumulation of power is the object of political man, Machiavelli adds that "it cannot be called virtue to kill one's fellow-citizens, betray one's friends, be without faith, without pity, and without religion; by these methods one may indeed gain power but not glory."[12]

In evaluating power as a means of achieving the agreement that the public seeks and needs, it may help to recall Peirce's discussion of the different bases of belief. He dismissed several bases as insecure and unreliable because they include no pragmatic link to the real world. The same kind of problem confronts the use of power, the problem of "might makes right." The fact that the person subjected to power is forced to conform or go along in some way with the powerful, yet not have any commitment of belief or will, suggests that power contains the seeds of its own dissolution, that it is not, in Dewey's sense, satisfactory; it *will* not do. The weakness of power is that the results it produces may not —likely will not—have continually satisfying effects. Those who may assert the rightness of public goals on the basis of their power to assert them are analogous to those who believe all variety of absurdities out of tenacity and stubbornness. Indeed, this is precisely why it is often thought that real strength of leadership is exhibited to the extent that the threat of power can be muted or avoided in the first place, and most unmitigated uses of power reveal its natural fragility. When a real test of power is unavoidable, the many underlying frictions and disagreements may tear apart the very fabric of power relationships. The increase in the role that power plays in developing conjoint public action would seem to decrease the stability, reliability, and satisfactoriness over time of the public's ends.

Though the three methods considered so far each play a vital role in the resolution of various kinds of human conflicts, none seems to constitute a satisfying resolution of the problem at hand. Indeed, all of these approaches seem to base their appeal on considerations drawn from outside the realm of political action. Spontaneity, at least in its liberal form, seems to be a response to the demands of individualism and voluntarism; rational proof seems designed to meet the exigencies of science and philosophy; and the power approach seems to grow out of attempts to bring man's social life into line with "realistic" views of his natural aggressiveness and competitiveness. The inadequacy of these approaches suggests that in looking for a mode of establishing public beliefs about ends, we ought not to look at man as a willful individual, a rational knower, or an aggressive animal, but as a social actor.

This does not deny that agreements about public ends can be and indeed are reached by such means, just as with beliefs in general the real issue concerning public purposes is whether there is some fairly reliable, intelligible means of justifying them such that they will continue to work for man and grow as fuller and more desirable responses of the public to its problems. The problem of justification requires that the mode of agreement be such that it includes public assent as a continual corrective to affirmations of the public good. In other words, pragmatically, the test of beliefs is their workability and the test of claims to the public interest is the satisfactoriness that the public finds in them. Within the approaches mentioned are helpful suggestions that lead toward a possible answer. The argument for rational proof includes the idea that people's beliefs change, that the change can put one person's beliefs into agreement with another's, and that the change can be effected by demonstrations and arguments that are the product of human shaping and control. Also, the actual operation of rational proof seen as a social transaction is itself a case of influence— that is, *A* gets *B* to do something he would not otherwise do. This suggests that a proper mode of agreement would consist of some variety of the larger phenomenon of human influence.

The normal events of social life continually display a mode of agreement, unlike the ones that have been mentioned, that would appear to be the type of human influence we are looking for. Indeed, it is such an ordinary and conventional kind of social relationship that it may easily be passed over for its obviousness. If we examine individuals in groups and try to trace their conjoint action to its source, quite commonly we discover the influence of a leader, one who takes the initiative, steps out ahead of others, and shows the way. We find people assenting to the leadership of others, not because the leader has proven something, but because of the compelling attractiveness and inspiration of the leader's line of action. The leader challenges uncertainty by offering a clear direction; in the amorphous context of indecision, the clarity of his articulation is influential; his character, past performances and arts of communication become his resources. He demonstrates through the force of his own will and effort that he has a positive good to offer; he gains the assent of people. Though this phenomenon has historically taken a variety of forms, in an empirical and generic sense it is the essence of what men have called *authority*.

Bertrand de Jouvenel, who has perhaps described it best, sees authority as "the faculty of gaining another man's assent"; it is "the ability of a man to get his own proposals accepted." Authority is a kind of influence, but a kind that is accepted and adopted voluntarily, as a result of the efforts of the one who leads. De Jouvenel speaks of the "daily spectacle . . . of man leading man on, of the ascendency of a settled will which summons and orients uncertain wills,"[13] and his description of this suggests a very pragmatic kind of process:

The process of formation gets into gear through the initiative of a single man, who sows among others the seed of his purpose; some of them, in whom it rises, turn into a small group of apostles

for the scheme and these form the nucleus that preaches and re-
cruits. Each of them influences others, whose interest they arouse,
whose support is progressively won. At length the association
comes into being, not by a mere coincidence of wishes, but as the
fruit of one man working on another.[14]

Authority historically takes on many different forms and guises;
and the ways in which authority becomes structured, institutionalized, altered, and variously ingrained into the mind of social man
constitute an important topic for political inquiry. But consider
how this rudimentary conception of authority allows us to account
for how the public can operate to make intelligible, conjoint determinations about its collective good. First, authority pays recognition to the basic uncertainty about public goals by not presuming
to achieve assent through the demonstrated proof of some settled
truth. Instead, it promotes beliefs as plausible "hypotheses" for
the public to act upon precisely because of the lack of ends blessed
by intellectual certitude; public authority provides an orderly direction and purpose through which the ultimate test of experience
can be set in motion. Authority suggests how the public may act
without any prior certainty about ends but with, instead, a commitment to a promising direction to be explored. On the other
hand, authority is also responsive to the need for action. As we
saw, the calls for rational proof of public ends or for spontaneous
agreement run against the exigencies of public action. Authority,
on the contrary, can not only operate effectively where the need
to act becomes demanding, but it often flourishes the most in such
situations. The personal and primitive kind of authority described
above often reveals itself at moments of crisis, where leadership
is called for, to deal with those genuine options that will not wait.
But aside from dramatic exhibitions of authority, the point is that
this manner of group agreement is not based on any conditions,
beyond the capacity to shape agreement out of public speech and
action, that would induce withdrawal from genuine options.

Not only does authority operate within the bounds of the
public's special dilemma, but it also constructs agreement in a
form amenable to the pragmatic test of belief. The way in which
this happens is twofold. First, and most obviously, by consisting
essentially of the "gaining of assent," authoritative action is submitted to the test of popular will. Claims resting on authority
rather than power are put in a form in which the practical success
of the claim may be directly tied to whether or not it does in fact,

represent what people want. Actual convergence of these two things will, of course, greatly depend on the articulateness and vigor of public expression. Pragmatically, claims to the public good must work, and one way in which they must work is through their effectivenesses in directing the public's energies. Dependence on authority continually involves the examination of such effectiveness.

However, these claims must work not only in the sense of successfully achieving assent as a result of their promotion, but also in the sense of generating concretely satisfying consequences. In this second sense, the mode of authoritative agreement rests on the satisfactoriness of the results it leads to; in the final analysis, it always comes down to that. The more fully claims are rooted in articulate authority, the more they are put on solid pragmatic grounds for the settlement of their value. Despite all attempts to embellish one's authority with the gloss of revealed truth, the loss of its pragmatic value and its popular abandonment make of it stuff for academic philosophy (possibly waiting in the wings to be reborn in the world of action) or else historical artifact. The abstract idea of the public good is brought to life in man's experience by this particular fact of social behavior, that people can and do purposefully act together not out of capricious coincidence, threat of coercion, or rational proof of proper ends, but out of the influence of those who provide direction and purpose by the example of their own action and speech through which they become the guarantor, the promoter, the instigator, the "man whose advice is followed," the one "who vouches for the success of the enterprise."[15] The fact that so many social enterprises work, indeed that they arise in the first place, can only be understood in terms of such a process.

Given the fundamental reality of the public conditions of life generated as effects of man's basic social interactions, given the pressing alternatives for regulation and control with which these conditions confront the members of the public, and given the lack of any *a priori* certitude about what is to be done, when asked how we can account for the public arriving at any determinations about the public good in an intelligible, human way, in line with our understanding of what constitutes true beliefs, the answer can be found in the phenomenon of authority, the medium of the public's successful operation, the device by which social order is created through the peculiarly human faculties of speech and action.

Authority is the pragmatic approach operating in the realm of public beliefs and it makes of the public good a determinable, sensible assertion in the realm of concrete, human experience.

Some difficulties are encountered because so far we have viewed the public more in terms of the problem of its identity, whereas now we are viewing the public in relation to the problem of action. It would be a mistake to think that the public literally acts as a unanimous and collective agent with the articulateness and singleness of a person. But if this is not the case, are we not confronted with the dangerous situation of different factions in society, each trying to present itself as the only authentic spokesman of the public? We should keep in mind that the problem of a part acting for the whole is a ubiquitous problem of politics; it is not a new problem that arises from the theory of the public interest. Indeed, it may only appear to arise in this way because such a theory attempts to deal with the part/whole problem directly. There is no essential reason why the fact that a part of the society presumes to speak for the whole should disturb us; what is disturbing is the feeling that we have no way to appraise such claims in relation to the needs of the public and that such appraisals do not appear vital to politics. The public does not act for itself in some unmediated way, but the existence of the public gives meaning to the idea of "public acts." Such acts address matters of public affairs in appropriately public terms and with results that can be evaluated for their public ramifications. The idea of authority helps us to see how a part can be a valid instrument of the whole, and in this respect a vital aspect of authority is that it is strengthened precisely insofar as it becomes more widely accepted and insofar as that acceptance is rooted in pragmatically well-founded beliefs.

If we reject the idea of the public as literally involved in collective, unified action, we still wish to speak of politics in the public interest as a pragmatic form of politics, grounded in the experience of the members of the public and operating through political authority. In considering what this means for democracy, a good deal of confusion has to do with the abuse of the concept of authority, its pejorative connotation for liberal democrats, and the unfortunately narrow attitude about the concept resulting from contemporary concern with the phenomenon of "authoritarianism." A refreshing commentary on this confusion is offered by Giovanni Sartori who, in raising the issue of "what democracy is not," citticizes the conventional antithesis between democracy and authority, noting that the two "are so interwoven that we can hardly speak of democracy without speaking of authority," and that "democracy typically requires power as authority."[16] Isaiah Berlin also presents a position that challenges the conventional wisdom in rejecting the positivist/technocratic approach to twentieth-century political organization, arguing that, in fact, the reliance on political authority more accurately reflects the tentativeness and probabilism of political ends and programs. Authority must be the guide: "Since no solution can be guaranteed against error, no disposition is final."[17]

The point is that political authority is not undemocratic. Indeed, it is almost commonsensical that democracy itself, as a mode of conducting public affairs in the most widely satisfactory way, will work as a form of decision-making only when it is authoritatively accepted; an operational system of democratic decision-making is itself an authority structure. Moreover, a leader-follower relationship is more inevitably characteristic of power relations than of authority relations. We may be misled on this score because of the phenomenon of diffuse, pluralistic, non-hierarchical power systems, yet such systems do not represent any abandonment of the leader-follower transactions but only an abandonment of the unified, directed coordination of power. Thus, the free market system, as a system of balancing economic power, always results in the division of those who more or less have power and those who more or less do not. Power, using the Dahl model, by definition divides society into haves and have nots, irrespective of its arrangement in the society; this is why the slogan "power to the people" is literally nonsensical. The key element of authority is the element of "right" and this changes the whole character of things because it presumes at the very minimum that the "follower" is one who, in some way or another, has partaken of the creation and definition of authority. Robert Nisbet, asserting that the real problem of modern society is not the poor arrangement of power but the weakness of authority, notes that "authority, like power, is a form of constraint, but, unlike power, it is based ultimately upon the consent of those under it: that is, it is conditional."[18] Authority is successfully operative because the leader-follower relation is not a one-way, command relation. Indeed, in the case of authority there really are no "mere followers," for the mere following of authority is itself indicative of the fragile condition of authority.

What intimidates the democrat about authority is the idea of an elite that has authority, but this only results from the mistaken notion that democracy requires utter directionlessness or leaderlessness. If we accept the assumption that democracies require leaders, surely we would want those leaders to be possessed of some authority. Furthermore, if the essence of democracy is that "the people rule," then the notion of rulership and all that it implies is contained in the very definition of democracy. The task of democracy is not to dissemble the art and function of governance—that is the task of anarchy; rather, it is to popularly manage governance. As long as we presume that when we speak of democracy we speak of a system of government, we must still deal with the problem of direction and control; the implication of the present argument is that only through the instrument of authority can we begin to imagine a defensible conception not only of how the public interest can be determined, but also of how that determination can occur democratically. What should intimidate the democrat, rather than the fact of political leadership, is the lack of popular mechanisms for shaping and controlling the authority embodied in leadership. This link between the people and public authority is described by Jacques Maritain:

What I mean is that it is not enough to define a democratic society by its legal structure. Another element plays also a basic part, namely the dynamic leaven or energy which fosters political *movement,* and which cannot be inscribed in any constitution or embodied in any institution, since it is both personal and contingent in nature, and rooted in free initiative. I should like to call that existential factor a prophetic factor. Democracy cannot do without it. . . .

In the normal functioning of a democratic society the political animation thus proceeds from men who, feeling themselves designated for a vocation of leadership, follow the usual channels of political activity—they will become chiefs of political parties, they will come to power through the legal machinery of elections. The happiest circumstance for the body politic obtains when the top men in the state are at the same time genuine prophets of the people.[19]

Authority gives to the public its "political animation" such that the public is no longer seen merely as a group identified by objective conditions or by legal category; rather, through such identity, the public relates to action as the arena or stage of politics. The insistence that the idea of the public as a real group must impose on us the conception of the public as collective agent is an excessively rationalist imposition; from the present point of view, the significance of the public as it relates to action is not the thoroughgoing politicization of each and every member, but simply the fact that the identity of the public defines what political action is all about and lays it open for all. Democracy adds to this the attempt to raise this public responsibility and granting of authority to a more conscious institutional and ideological level such that the citizen can see authority at work, see his part in it, and see his accountability for it.

Though we have dwelt on authority in its most rudimentary form and though much is still to be said about the analysis of the workings of authority, it is possible at this point to lay down the bare essentials of the concept of the public good: the public good consists of those authoritative values that satisfactorily direct a society in its response to the problems of the public in such a way as to relieve the largest amount of doubts about the rightness of the public's purposes. The public good is thus a fluid and dynamic historical phenomenon, perhaps the most fundamental phenomenon of man's political history. The essential value of this conception is the new dimensions it opens up for political analysis; since the concept has been presented in its general, theoretical form, what now must be looked into are its interesting and valuable ramifications for our accounts of the political world.

NOTES

1. Sidney Hook explains: "Similarly, one can tell whether he shares the same idea with another person to whom one is speaking ultimately only in terms of the possibility of conjoint behavior between them in concrete situations. You understand me well to the extent that you intelligently co-operate with or obstruct my purposes." Hook, p. 152.
2. John Dewey, *The Quest for Certainty*, p. 26.
3. Dewey, *Quest*, pp. 22–23.
4. Hannah Arendt, *Between Past and Future*, p. 114.

5. See V. I. Lenin, pp. 31–53.
6. Friedrich A. Hayek, pp. 59–60.
7. Jean-Jacques Rousseau, p. 269.
8. Isaiah Berlin summarizes the common spirit of these several currents: "Man is, in principle at least, everywhere and in every condition, able, if he wills it, to discover and apply rational solutions to his problems. And these solutions, because they are rational, cannot clash with one another, and will ultimately form a harmonious system in which the truth will prevail, and freedom, happiness and unlimited opportunity for untrammelled self-development will be open to all." Berlin, *Four Essays on Liberty*, p. 8.
9. Robert A. Dahl, p. 40.
10. Dahl, p. 50.
11. Niccolo Machiavelli, p. 38.
12. Machiavelli, p. 32.
13. Betrand de Jouvenel, pp. 29–31.
14. de Jouvenel, p. 28.
15. de Jouvenel, p. 30.
16. Giovanni Sartori, pp. 138–139.
17. Berlin, *Four Essays*, p. 40.
18. Robert A. Nisbet, p. xiii.
19. Jacques Maritain, pp. 139–140.

CHAPTER TEN

THE PUBLIC INTEREST
RECONSIDERED

The problem we are attempting to close in on is how it can be said that the public, which we have empirically identified, is able to make determinations about the proper regulation and control of public business in such a way that these determinations can properly and legitimately be called the good of the public. To this point, the search for an answer has led to a combination of the pragmatic theory of the truth and goodness of beliefs in general with the phenomenon of authority as a method of arriving at public agreement that conforms to the conditions of the pragmatic theory of truth. In order to elaborate this relationship and show how it makes possible an empirical and logical theory of the public good, it is necessary to look more closely into the phenomenon of authority and some of the critical issues it raises.

The first point of clarification is that authority in the political world usually manifests itself in much more stable and formal ways than is suggested by de Jouvenel's comments. The characterization of authority as "gaining assent" represents only the most primal and essential component of the larger, intricate historical phenomenon, and this conception has been used so far only to suggest how authority, as a mode of agreement among men, possesses all the necessary attributes to satisfy a pragmatic account of how the public conducts its business. One of the first concerns of political man is to create a stable, reliable foundation for authority. The original responses to the influence of the leader become regularized, patterned, predictable, such that each new event or crisis does not require a complete replaying of the original premise of authority. Politics thus becomes smoother and more reliable, more stable and secure; a certain political order takes shape and this orderliness is essential for political man to establish some control over the unpredictable future. The public beliefs that come to act as consistent guides to public action form what may be called the *authority structure* of the society, which most closely resembles what Gaetano Mosca identified as the "juridical defense" of a society.[1]

The authority structures that have developed through history are numerous and varied. Authority may be thought to be embodied in an individual, a hereditary line, a ruling class; possibly it will take the form of a written document or certain basic principles that form a "constitution." But whatever the device, in any established political order one can discover some root public principle of right that has become settled upon, that constitutes the existing set of beliefs upon which the public develops its response to the need to regulate public affairs. Thus, just as the dynamics of truth-seeking take place within a concrete context of existing beliefs that are not at the moment under question, so too the dynamics of authority in its original and essential manifestation take place within the framework of an authority structure already laid down, already at work.

Study of the meaning of the public good for particular societies can then begin with an analysis of the society's authority structure, the existing pattern of authoritative values, the public's beliefs. This structure can be examined through an empirical study of the attitudes and beliefs prevalent in the society, yet the real test is the actual response generated by political appeal to authoritative values. In the United States, for example, authoritative principles make possible the daily conduct of political business: the belief that public policies ought to be constitutional, that certain official positions ought to be filled by popular election, that opposition to public policies ought to be pursued through appeals addressed to particular governmental arenas or to political parties, etc. Though the authority structure of the United States, by virtue of its liberal roots, seems to display greater concern for the procedures of politics, it is by no means limited to this and it equally includes such beliefs as the following: economic transactions ought to be generally subject to the supply and demand of the market, with occasional specific regulation of such transactions allowable to broaden economic opportunity, achieve greater stability, or remedy severe injustices. Very little public debate in America gets outside such a formulation on the matter of economics.

It may be observed that the collection of principles that have been called the authority structure rest to a great extent on habitual, well-socialized responses that do not reflect a real attentiveness to the public good. This is true, yet the issue of whether or not assent is conscious and well thought out does not affect the fact that beliefs are authoritative; what it may affect is the vigor and strength of commitment to authority, especially under pressure. The individual, like the public, possesses many beliefs that often are not questioned, that operate on a daily basis as habitual responses, and this static quality of beliefs may be a mark of their general usefulness and a response to the need for regularity and continuity in life so that routine events do not continually cause confusion and indirection. The important point is that existing beliefs, whether habitual or not, are always subject to the challenge of experience.

If in any society there are certain matters about which authority has become firmly settled, there are also other matters about which there is no authoritative response, intensive conflict over what the correct response ought to be, or no felt need to generate a response. Analysis, thus, turns from a consideration of the static form of authority to the dynamics of authority, the ways in which it is altered, molded, expanded, and reshaped as a result of the pressures on, and challenges to, established authority resulting from the limitedness of what stability it has, its incompleteness, its lack of perfection and finality and, if nothing else, the changing character of public problems. The relative and incomplete character of the existing authority structure invites new, alternative claims to the public good, claims intended to satisfy doubts about the continuing effectiveness and satisfactoriness of present directions. The dynamics of authority tear man away from habitual ways of thinking and bring back a feeling of the original and primal mode of authority that was so personal. As we have seen, contemporary analysis tends to view such challenging claims to the public good as rhetorical devices that hide more concrete, material motives unrelated to the public good. This raises an interesting line of questioning: why would we expect such an appeal to have such influence in the first place? And if the appeal is made and does influence people, does it not establish certain expectations, and would not these expectations become concrete limitations in the future? Does not experience itself become a check on the seriousness of such claims and is their constant use as mere rhetorical devices the source of political frustration and disenchantment? Whether or not claims to the public good are made in a frivolous and self-serving way, if one wishes to treat them seriously they must be taken as a practical hypothesis. For example, "If the public will agree to adopt this new value or set of values for the purpose of shaping its response to public problems, the general conditions of public affairs will be more satisfying, it will allow for the fulfillment of an even more expansive 'best whole' of goods." This type of claim does not occur in a vacuum; it is offered within a concrete context of existing values, of problems to which existing values may not adequately respond, and of the society's past, which marks its record of successes and failures.

The fate of challenges to existing conceptions of the public good will be determined by the workings of political practice put to the task of making these challenges authoritative. The new values become the basis for establishing new leadership; political leadership suggests, initiates, promotes the values and its vehicle is its ability to generate trust and confidence, which in turn will come through the plausibility and "liveness" of the new value options themselves, combined with the strength of the past record of those who are leading as authorities to be followed. The leader leads because of his successes. The dynamic processes that sort out competing claims to the public good find a resting place, though temporary, in the confirmation of existing values, a change in these values, or some additive expansion or embellishment of them. Like the processes of thought that consist of the dynamic relationship between our beliefs and our doubts, the operations of authority within a public resemble a pulsating continuing movement from a point of rest to activity and back again. How a society deals with the dynamics of authority, how it gives shape and direction to these dynamics, the conditions of social action and communication that affect authority, the degree to which its public life encourages or discourages the workings of political authority, constitute perhaps the main topic that political science should consider. A critical difference among political systems consists of the different ways in which they manage the dynamics of authority in pursuit of the public good. Much of contemporary political analysis has directed its energies toward an understanding of political events occurring within a particular given framework of authority, but the most fundamental understanding of what is happening in politics requires greater inquiry into the very ground of man's political experience, the vital factor that allows ordinary, conventional politics to take place at all, the authoritative public good.

One result of the view taken here is that the actual content of the public good is transitory. The two most obvious reasons for this are that, 1) since even an accepted claim to the public good would be hypothetical, it may require alteration or even abandonment as a result of being tested and, 2) indirect consequences themselves are always subject to change, which would lead to changes in the conception of the public good. Though a great deal of flux in the content of the public good could be a difficulty as the issue becomes more specific, and though it is clearly the intention of the argument to dismiss the notion of any permanent and fixed public good, nevertheless much of what we can descriptively identify as beliefs that effectively constitute the public good are by no means ephemeral. In looking at the static and dynamic features of authority, it should be noted that what is usually more permanent are vague and general beliefs, while problems of settling authoritative claims often concern more specific matters.

Authority addresses itself not only to values but also to explanations and descriptions of the world. Thus, an authoritative claim not only involves the assertion that a given policy is good or better than alternatives but that it will, in fact, generate a particular set of consequences. Political activity built around concern for the public good takes the form of promoting certain claims as, in essence, social hypotheses, propositions about what could or will work and could be or will be more satisfactory. Will it work better to view the world as a bi-polar struggle, a multi-polar struggle, or not in terms of struggle at all? Will it work better to operate on the assumption that crime is rooted in socio-economic conditions or in the generally loose morals of society? Are we to find greater economic stability and security in allowing the marketplace completely unfettered operation or in imposing certain regulations; or do we want economic security more than individual economic independence? The fact is that one way or another these kinds of matters are settled; the behavior of those in official positions in the state—the organized instrument of the public—manifests such settlements. And, as was seen, there are many ways of settling the issue, only one of which is through authority, and, indeed, where authority is not possible because of the polarization of views in the society, other means will be used or a settlement will perhaps be avoided and, in fact, can be if a genuine option is not at stake. But where the settlement occurs as the result of an exercise in authority, where public promotion and initiation, evaluation of the problem, and appraisal of the past performances of leaders and policies takes place, and where the guidance of pragmatic consequences is dominant, then the official position can be said to constitute not merely an opinion or power claim about the public good, but a testable assertion of it.

This portrayal of the relationship between the workings of authority and the identification of the public good raises a number of classical theoretical issues that must be dealt with. We might begin by considering the distinction between what people *want* and what people *need,* a distinction that often implies the kind of opposition between objective values and subjective impulses that pragmatism tends to avoid. Classical Greek thought was very critical of democracy on the basis that popular rule would subject politics to the raw passions of the people; it would serve their wants and ignore their needs as understood by elites sufficiently wise or informed to know what those needs are. The volatile expressions of the masses in modern times have been the cause of similar reactions on the part of such people as Edmund Burke, Joseph de Maistre and Alexander Hamilton, and this conservative reaction has been countered by the resistance of the individualistic, liberal citizen to the idea that someone in power can declare what is good for him. It may thus be asked whether this account of the public good is supposed to tell us about what the public wants or what it needs.

Within the framework of pragmatic theory, the noun "want" would refer to an existing belief in a value. Like any belief, it may be arrived at and held in a variety of ways and it exhibits itself through the consequences of action. It may be carefully analyzed, closely attended to and continually re-examined, or it may be merely automatic, habitual, and tenacious. In any event, to say that someone wants something is merely to state a fact. A "need," on the other hand, suggests not merely the fact that something is desired or wanted, but that the want can be or has been subjected to some kind of justification; pragmatically speaking, a need is identified where the expectations of the good that will result from pursuit of what one wants are confirmed or denied by concrete experience.

Thus, in asking whether the discussion of the public good concerns wants or needs, the answer is that it concerns both. On one level the public good represents what people want through the assent that sustains established authority, but, though this may be a legitimate view, it may also be trivial. The real question of importance is how a public is able to put its view of the public good on a secure and justifiable basis—that is, how wants can be translated into needs or rejected in favor of needs. Wants are what people think they need, and needs are what people want once they are known. The process that is of interest here is the process through which men come to accept certain things as needs, and how that process works well or poorly for the affairs of the public. It is interesting to note in this respect that even Plato, despite the larger superstructure of his philosophical idealism, finally confronts Glaucon and Adeimantus towards the end of the *Republic* with a concrete, pragmatic appreciation for the likely inadequacy of appetitive wants and the larger satisfaction one will experience with a more expansive view of human needs.[2] He seeks to seal his case for justice by asking for a "a report on the happiness or misery of the despot as compared with the rest of the world."[3]

Also considered important to any discussion of authority is the distinction between *de facto* and *de jure* authority. The view of authority developed here is analytical and descriptive; it attempts to account for *de facto* authority. People really do gain others' assent through their speech and action; agreements are really molded in this fashion and used as the basis for group policy; and the strength and the duration of this authority is historically subject to the pragmatic test of experience. Far from being mysterious, authority is the commonplace fuel of collective social action rooted in the leader's ability to make claims and convince people of their worth, to make promises and then fulfill them. Authority, in this sense, can be said to be at work whenever the public is convinced by the declaration that an act is proper and acceptable because it is constitutional or is the will of the prince or is in conformity with Marxist theory, etc. But this phenomenon of authority necessarily raises the issue of the distinction between *de facto* and *de jure* authority. It is true, in fact, that societies develop a certain authority structure and that they change in certain ways, but is there any basis for saying that these actual manifestations of authority ought to be followed and obeyed? It is worth noting that we do not usually apply any parallel distinction in speaking of personal moral beliefs because of the modern secular view that all moral imperatives emanate from individual conscience; thus, my actual moral beliefs are what I ought to obey. In fact, the same is true of those members of society who accept authority, who are in voluntary concurrence with it; they ought to obey society because they believe in it. *De facto* authority for them is *de jure*. Therefore, the problem of *de jure* authority is really a corollary to a more fundamental problem, what might be called the problem of unanimity: if the public is a large all-inclusive grouping bound together by the indirect consequences of social relations, why should those members of the public obey who are in disagreement with the mainstream of established authority that has, in fact, come into operation without benefit of their assent? Does *de jure* authority require unanimity?

This issue probably represents the heart of the resistance to the idea that there can be a public interest. It may not be so much the difficulty of admitting the existence of public problems, nor that these problems generate genuine options, nor that, in some way, through politics these options can be decided upon. What is disturbing is the idea that a society's response to these problems can in any legitimate way be called the expression of that group known as the public. The problem is that if the public is not truly speaking, but only a part of the public, which is able to prevail through control of the coercive instruments of the state, then we are thrown back on "agreements" established through power, a mode that was rejected earlier. To deal with this problem, the discussion must first be rid of a false issue. The problem of one part of society defining the public good for the whole society is often perceived as a problem of "man versus the state." In other words, the fact that a part of society can impose its view of the public good is seen as a limitation and coercion of the individual in his attempt to control his own life. In response to this view, the first point is that the extent of individual autonomy is not necessarily limited by the mere fact of an established official view of the public good, but by the content of that view. If we focus on the content of authority, it will be noted that political authority may be coercive but it may also promote, and perhaps be the only real guarantee of, the right to individual control over private affairs and protection of all the basic liberal rights that insure the opportunity for the expression of opposite political points of view.

Even given authoritative support for limited government and individual rights, it may still be contended that individual autonomy is violated by the notion that public authority supported by assent from less than the whole public ought to be obeyed by the whole public.[4] But it is very misleading to frame the issue in this way, for if we trace the limitations on individual autonomy back to their source we find that they originate not with authority, but with the coercive influence of those indirect consequences that define public problems; they do not derive originally from the actions of the state but from the conditions to which the state is responding. To a great extent a certain individualistic fetish is an obstacle to an appreciation of this fundamental situation; and we need not commit ourselves wholesale to a Hobbesian "state of war" premise to make the simple observation that the forces of public authority can be useful in freeing man from the forces of nature and of unregulated human transactions. Public authority, through the regulation and control that it pursues, does not create limitations on man but substitutes one set of limitations for another. Before civil rights legislation, certain people were limited in what housing they could rent or buy; now certain other people are limited in their control over deciding to whom their house can be rented or sold. If the issue is couched in terms of individual self-determination, then the issue is moot. Non-concurrence with authority based on limitations on the individual is not a convincing basis for impugning the rightness of public authority or for denying any obligation to obey; after all, the task of public authority by definition concerns *social* problems, not *individual* problems. This is not even to mention that the individualistic position often leaves very muddled the idea of what individualistic self-determination is supposed to mean in the first place. Thus, the real issue of the lack of unanimity and the obligations of dissenters concerns those alternative dissenting claims to the public good. The real problem is not man versus the state, but different proposed goals for the public versus established goals and directions. Only authority can establish obligation, for only authority addresses itself to what is right in the conduct of the public's business, and therefore the issue becomes why one should obey a claim to the public good different from his own claim to the public good.

Having pared the issue to its meaningful essentials, it can be said only that one ought to obey the authoritative view of the public good as opposed to his own view of it—that authority is *de jure*—on the condition that the consequences of obedience would, in his best judgment, yield a greater good *for the public*. This pragmatic case for obedience points to the fact that disobedience itself may damage the possibility for effective public action of any sort and for the smooth and civil determination of public goals; disobedience is a challenge not only to public policy but to the very integrity of the means by which the public conducts its business. Disobedience is not justified merely because of disagreement with policy, but only because it presents itself as the only pragmatic way to respond to the total picture of public action, including the existing condition of public problems, the quality of various alternative solutions, their chances of being proved more valuable than the established solution, and the quality and usefulness of the mechanisms of public debate and decision-making. Pragmatically, the issue of obedience does not turn on particular policies but on the consequences of disobedience for the total conduct of the public's business. Indeed, the positive good of disobedience in certain situations, as Martin Luther King so incisively understood, derives from the timeliness and public drama of the act, which allows the public to see in vivid fashion and at the critical moment the deficiences in the conduct of its business. Just as in the general pragmatic approach to the problem of values, *de jure* authority is not created by ethical philosophy but comes into reality only through the social experiences of man, we are obliged to follow authority on the same basis that we are obliged to pursue the good in general, because it works and will continue to work to the largest satisfaction. It should also be noted that the pragmatic statement of the obligation to obey refers to yielding a greater good *for the public*. This is an important condition because the premise of the argument is that we are talking about the public's business, and the weight of decision turns, not directly on the pragmatic consequences for the individual, but on what this augurs for the public, which is why the most telling and troubling plea of the oppressed is, "If they can do it to me, they can do it to anyone." In the context of everyone's fate obligation must be established.

Another problem raised by the probable lack of complete unanimity of assent is whether or not it is presumptuous to refer to authoritative settlements as the *public* interest, which suggests the image of the public speaking in massive unison. It should be noted that when we use the term *private* interests, we apply it to overt, concrete behavioral manifestations of interest and do not feel it necessary, for the legitimate application of the term, to consider the individual's internal conflicts and misgivings. His vote, which may be used to identify his interests, may have been arrived at through a painful search of conscience, which may not be really settled even after his decision is revealed. Indeed, despite the lack of unanimity, we even use the term in this way when referring to the decisions of private groups; formal announcements of decisions and actions that are taken become the interest of that particular group. It would seem legitimate and consistent, therefore, to use the designation "public" in referring to the interests manifested in the operation of public business through the offices of the state. This is not to contend that every action of the state will be proved to be in the public good or, for that matter, as we will see, that every action is even directly authoritative; what it simply means is that the proper use of the term *public* need not depend on the mere fact of complete unanimity.

What must now be done is to look, in summary fashion, at the kind of response that has been developed to those who have been critical, for various reasons, of the idea of the public interest. Building on an empirical conception of the public, and the analytical conceptualization of the public interest, as referring, in its general sense, to those affairs that are the proper business of the public, and given that these affairs present to the public various options for their regulation and control that exhibit the features of what James calls "genuine options," with all of the pragmatic ramifications such options have for human decisions and action, the problem was how it was possible to speak of the public making decisions and taking actions about such regulation and control and be able legitimately to call such determinations the public good. The approach of philosophical pragmatism was adopted as the only approach that really made possible an analytical account of the public interest, and its adaptability was seen to result from the fact that it treats the problems of human knowledge within an existential context peculiarly relevant to the dilemma in which the public finds itself. Thus, the inquiry proceeded to lay out the pragmatic account of human beliefs about the true and the good with its distinctive principle of an experimental test, which weaves knowing and acting together in the process of removing concrete doubt and settling beliefs. In applying the pragmatic approach to the situation in which the public finds itself, it was argued that the mode of generating and sustaining conjoint action in such a way that goals can be subjected to the pragmatic mode of verification is found in the method of developing and establishing authority. The understanding of the way in which a society goes about settling upon a particular conception of the public good, and what the worth of that conception is, requires investigation into the working of political authority and the various ways a society goes about managing authority, including its growth, adjustment, petrification through time, institutionalization, adaptability to change, and the existing processes for change. In the simplest sense, the determination of the public good in practice occurs through the growth, establishment, and nurturing of political authority. As for the political scientist's role, his interest is surely in the processes of such determination and in the issue, both speculative and analytical, of what might or could constitute a workable formulation of the public interest in pragmatic terms. This approach pays recognition to the elusive, tenuous, and problematic character of any determinations about the public good, but though the problems of verification are at a higher order of magnitude than rather simple, immediate empirical confirmations, it is still a form of human belief subject to the same considerations as any other type of belief. And if it is supposed that the pragmatic principle of the meaning of truth seems a weak, ephemeral, perhaps too subjective basis on which to forage ahead with assertions about the public good, we should more seriously consider whether or not what is supposed to be our most concrete and immediate knowledge of the world is really based on anything more or anything less.

It may be argued that although we have woven an interesting abstract design, the bulk of phenomena we call political hardly reflects daily concern with these matters and that despite empirical and logical support for the public interest idea, the theoretical view presented here does not effectively touch base with the brute facts of political life. However, we are concerned not merely with getting in touch with the brute facts of political life but with understanding them. If politics does not really go on in this way, we may want to know why it does not and what the ramifications are. Like any theory, it ought to suggest the things we ought to look for, the questions we ought to ask in order to find out what is really going on, and this assumes that understanding does not leap out at us from the brute facts. Why is it, for example, that in a political system like that of the United States, which is so free, open, and representative, there are so many displays of political impotence, frustration, and alienation? How much will the brute facts tell us about that problem? We should recall that for William James and Josiah Royce, the level of our understanding was seen to be greatly controlled by the scope and breadth of our attention and the crucial ability to move from the realm of immediate facts in the foreground of attention to the "rest of the universe" to things "out of sight" such that our world-views do not consist of what *is* but of what *might be, could be,* or *will be.*

Ultimately, the value of any theoretical paradigm, such as the one presented here, rests not on the strength of its theoretical underpinnings, but on its pragmatic value in offering better explanations and a greater general understanding of the political world. Though the conclusiveness of such tests tends to come only in the longer run, the last chapter is intended to identify some analytically useful lines of development for public interest theory, especially in relation to those criticisms mentioned at the outset.

NOTES

1. Gaetano Mosca, pp. 125–126.
2. See Plato, Chap. 33.
3. Plato, p. 303.
4. Robert Paul Wolff tries to make this case in *In Defense of Anarchism.* Wolff sets up individual autonomy as a value to which authority must conform and is thus led astray from the real issue, which is the general worth of authority as compared to the whole set of constraints men experience. Wolff eventually back-pedals and reaches, toward the end, the point at which he might have begun with the observation that "Man confronts a natural world that is irreducibly *other,* which stands over against him . . . ," p. 72.

CHAPTER ELEVEN

IMPLICATIONS
OF THE NEW PARADIGM

The point that we have reached in attempting to search out the meaning of the public good may strike many as a curious impasse. In returning to the fundamental question—"What is the public good?"—it is not at all clear that this inquiry can provide the kind of answers most people might expect. No list of worthy public values has been generated, no specific recipe or formula for public decision-makers can honestly be offered up. It would appear that little assistance is being given to political actors. Indeed, the approach taken here suggests that answers of this sort may be beyond the scope of political science or political theory. Indeed, the very presumption that the question might be neatly answered out of pure contemplation rather than thoughtful action and the cynicism evoked when this prospect remains unfulfilled is precisely what the present theory has tried to avoid. We are not prepared to substitute philosophy for politics. Social science can be most useful in posing hypothetical lines of action, tracing possible consequences, conceptually framing the requisites of political stability, and exposing and analyzing the human record of achievement and failure so as to inform the man of action; but the notion that social knowledge can replace social judgment and action has been profitless, dangerous, and suppressive. None of these confessed limitations of political theory, however, justifies the conclusion that the public good is empty, and to that theoretical challenge a substantial answer has been promoted. This concluding chapter is meant to suggest some analytical implications of the theory of the public good.

The conception of the public good promoted here is intended to be not only theoretically justifiable, but also analytically useful, or more correctly, justifiable because it is useful. It is useful not merely in the sense of telling us about political events in a systematic way but in the sense of allowing us to understand more effectively those events. Like any effective political theory, it must tell us about how things work in politics and also about how things do not work—"not work," that is, in terms of a conception of politics that may be beyond existing, operative ideological frameworks. As such, the public good is intended to be the focal point of several theoretical observations that suggest to us a constructive alternative to existing paradigms of political analysis.

Critically and analytically, the public good can be said to be the best regulation and control of the indirect consequences of social transactions as determined by the public through the satisfactoriness of actions it takes in pursuit of authoritative agreements about its goals. From this conceptualization, analysis of the public interest proceeds to a consideration of all of the variables involved. What values has the public authoritatively determined? What has been left undetermined? To what extent does politics manifest the conscious, open, critical appraisal of competing authoritative claims? To what extent is the existing authority structure satisfactory and workable? What sort of political methods assure the greatest continuity, stability, and success for the public in dealing with its affairs? How do challenges to authority begin, develop, and succeed or fail? What are the effects on a society of not attending to the development of the public good? Consistent with our purpose here, our intention is not to answer such questions, but to suggest that a proper understanding of the public interest concept opens up to political science a new perspective that should prove rich in what it tells us about our political life and in its ability to help our understanding of political crises and change.

In the first chapter it was observed that the product of intensive empirical and behavioral examination of American politics has generated a great deal of critical reaction from various quarters. Using the terminology of Thomas Kuhn,[1] political science dealing with the United States created a paradigm of competitive interest-group pluralism and, despite the invaluable insights it has produced about the workings of American politics, the paradigm has not been fully satisfactory. Yet if the criticisms of it are not to become moot, there must be an alternative paradigm that resolves doubts about the existing explanations of the world. The paradigm must deal with problems such as the following: If the system is free and open, and allows for peaceful change through participation based on group interests, why are there such negative feelings about politics, such frustration, and polarization that leads to intemperate volatile movements? If an authority structure already exists, how does it change, aside from changes that merely go on within the existing structure? What is the efficacy or usefulness of sincere claims that a particular value is in the public good? What are the consequences of ignoring claims at that level, and dealing with the affairs of the public through interest competition? Such analytical questions may be better dealt with through an appreciation of the concept of the public good and of the dynamics of authority that allow for its determination. In this chapter a few selective issues will be examined for the purpose of demonstrating the ramifications of public interest theory and showing some of the analytical uses to which it can be put.

It should be apparent by now that the present approach tends to see the public interest as *the political* problem that a society faces. In examining the determination of the public good through the dynamics of authority, those activities that are at the heart of what we call political will be discovered. This may be appreciated by looking at a common feature of the workings of authority: once a particular principle has become established as authoritative, it is then used as a referent for determining the rightness of further actions. This raises the analytical problem of distinguishing the immediate object of authority from those objects that merely derive some legitimacy from a certain connection with the immediate object. For example, taking the case in which a written constitution has become viewed as authoritative by a society, consider the following two statements: 1) we ought to allow trial by jury because the constitution requires it, and 2) we ought to allow trial by jury because it will be generally good for the society by contributing to a sense of justice and due process and by mitigating arbitrary action in the enforcement of laws by government. Notice that statement #1 is only indirectly a test of the legitimacy of trial by jury; it is essentially a test of the legitimacy of the constitution and would be meaningless without constitutional authority. Also, if constitutional authority happened to prohibit it, statement #1 implies that jury trials could just as easily be determined illegitimate. As was seen, the ability to determine such specifics from the general authority structure is quite important and basic because it provides for stable and continuous authority. However, the invoking of constitutional authority over time generates accumulated consequences that may not only help but also hinder the maintenance of original constitutional authority. This is because the legalism of statement #1 hides the political claim of statement #2, which is proposed as a direct test of the authoritativeness of jury trials. The first statement is a misleading solution to the problem of authority unless it is understood that, in the final analysis, it is not conformity to the constitution but the value of the practical consequences that will maintain authority. In the long run, the test suggested by the second statement will determine the viability of authority established by the first statement. The problem that authority must always contend with is the problem of striking a balance between rest and change—rest as typified by the invoking of the authority structure and change as typified by the expansion or circumvention of this structure through direct political appeals. It is necessary to have the continuity and stability offered by traditions and written laws, but there must also be some viable means of directly assessing claims to authority. If this balance is not cared for, one possible result could be that the carrying on of the public's business in an excessively legalistic form would stifle the possibility of directly widening and strengthening authority. In this way, authority is capable of becoming stagnant and tenuous even though grounded in the constitutional rule of law.

The distinction between direct and indirect claims to authority also helps in evaluating the contention that the public good is at best the result of some equilibrium or "vector-sum" of the struggle among interest groups as the result of open and fair political processes. As this contention is phrased, the results are presumably seen as legitimate because of the legitimacy that has developed for the group process. It may be said that such devices as popular elections, interest-based representation, bargaining, etc., are generally considered legitimate, but it is presumptuous to suggest that the results of such processes necessarily constitute the public good. Well-established, legitimate processes can go a long way in inducing the public to accept a variety of outcomes, yet the fact remains that the "vector-sum" of forces may not be in the public interest, and if it is not, it may cause the accumulation of frustration and ill will that may strike at the durability of political processes themselves. In a phrase, the statics of legal and procedural authority may stifle the dynamics of political authority, and it is the latter which keeps the public on course and allows creative adjustment to the public's problems. Institutionalized authority is merely a device at the service of politics, and it serves well when it provides a stable, orderly setting within which political action can go on.

This analysis suggests an important general hypothesis about politics: the more a society depends on existing authority structures for the justification of public acts without allowing for the expansion or alteration of that structure, the more the structure will become susceptible to being overloaded and its stability threatened. The importance of this hypothesis is that it suggests that the overload problem can occur with any kind of authority structure, whether it be liberal, representative, constitutional, legal, or despotic, aristocratic, or monarchical. A critical difference among authority structures is the extent to which they are responsive to the ultimate payoffs and consequences of public policies, which will determine the strength of public authority in the long run. This responsiveness requires the allowance of and support for free political action in pursuit of an expansion of authoritative directions and purposes. However, the most liberal system of rule under law is capable of this overloading, and such features as competitive elites or open competition among interest groups do not necessarily insure pragmatic responsiveness if the very framework of authority within which they operate cannot itself become the object of critical political action. Thus, what keeps rule of law and the free processes of group politics viable is not any inherent justice they may be claimed to possess, nor any logical proof of their rightness, nor the soundness of positivistic assumptions on which they may be based, but the continually satisfying consequences that they tend to produce. If such principles of political order fail to generate continually satisfying consequences, their justification may tend to dissolve. These observations may help us to understand better such classical dilemmas as the problem of majority tyranny. What if democratic majorities decide to tyrannize minorities? Theoretical focus on the public good draws attention to the more fundamental issue of why, in the first instance, the will of the majority ought to be authoritative. If politics is viewed as the activity of the public in search of its collective good, and if the criteria to be invoked are pragmatic, then the method of majority rule becomes a device that ought to be able to get the public to an adequate view of its purposes better than some other device. From this standpoint, the principle of majority rule has considerable merit, which may be enthusiastically accepted without challenging our consistency in refusing to tolerate majority tyranny.

Consistent with the idea of direct and indirect applications of authority and the overloading of existing authority structures John Schaar, in discussing the constitutionalist concept of equality, suggests certain helpful clarifications:

It should be especially emphasized that the constitutionalist approach, being formal, actually demands to be filled in by one of the other approaches, such as the equality of opportunity or utilitarian theories discussed above. The great virtue of the constitutionalist approach is precisely that of permissiveness. . . . No policy within these boundaries is illegitimate in principle; any policy accepted becomes, by the fact of its acceptance, legitimate.

It is important, however, if one would keep his thinking clear, not to equate "legitimate" with "justified." To say that a given public policy is legitimate is only to say that it does not conflict with the terms of the constitution. The justification for the policy rests on other grounds: religious, empirical, utilitarian, ethical, or some combination of these. The grounds themselves are neither supplied nor supported by the constitution.[2]

Yet there is some ground for the constitutional legitimacy of egalitarianism; that is, its justification is political. "The constitutionalists," explains Schaar, "have offered a specifically political way of thinking about equality. . . . Their everyman is a construct, not an empirical portrait, and it is a construct drawn for political ends. . . ."[3]

To be more precise in this line of analysis, the policies that are legitimized on the basis of the existing authority structure can be said to be authoritative only in a derivative sense. It might be said that such policies are endorsed by legal or constitutional authority, but it may be most accurate to reserve the term "political authority" for those claims directly tied to promised consequences for the public. Thus, the test of legal authority is whether the policy operates in such a way as to conform to the existing legal structure, yet political authority refers to claims tested in terms of the public appeal of those consequences promised or actually realized. This distinction provides an interesting perspective from which to examine the formation of public policies and their political ramifications. Consider, for example, the issue of racial integration in schools in the United States. What seems to have occurred is that policy about school integration has taken the form of an accumulation of highly particular, legal, and non-coordinated decisions mainly on the part of courts operating at various levels. The policy results were endowed with legal authority, yet these results met with intensive disagreement within the American public and therefore were seriously deficient because they were lacking in the direct authority that could only be provided by politics. The result has been that established authority became overloaded; it took on a policy problem it could not deal with—perhaps because of the failure of distinctly political structures—and the authority structure of the society was weakened as exhibited by the law-breaking and violence stimulated by court decisions on integration policies. Courts have been designed for the implementation of legal authority, and are not suited for dealing with political claims. The "equal protection of the law" that the courts might invoke in these cases is itself an originally political formulation, adopted because the cumulative results its application would lead to would presumably be better than the results of not having such equal protection. But what those results are constitutes itself an historical experiment; they are not known at the outset. And though the equal protection principle as a component of the structure of authority may be highly useful in the resolution of routine problems, if it is taken for granted or adopted with a legal dogmatism, it will imprudently and impractically be forced to carry the whole burden of unforeseen consequences, many of which will be ordinary enough but many of which will be controversial, if not ridiculous and bizarre. The task of politics is to regulate and control such consequences and this requires the continual revitalizing of authority through political determinations that transcend law. The authority structure is, after all, only a structure within which politics may go on; it is not a substitute for politics itself.

Standing behind the authority structure of the state is the ever-present though sometimes unconscious measure of pragmatic value, which recalls Aristotle's observation that "all men, as a rule, seek to follow, not the line of tradition, but some idea of the good."[4] This provides the basis for his advice that "the true end which good law-givers should keep in view, for any state or stock or society with which they may be concerned is the enjoyment of partnership in a good life and the felicity thereby attainable."[5]

This suggests that the highest claim that can be made to the public is not that a particular value is legal, constitutional, or procedurally correct, though all of these may have their weight; but the highest claim is that the value is in the public interest. This claim is the highest because it constitutes a direct, unmediated test of authority and its pragmatic confirmation can make irrelevant all other types of claims.

At this point we can also reconsider the proposition that American politics does not display concern for searching out some common good, but only seeks the practical and viable arrangement of political forces. Does this mean that the public interest is not a meaningful concept in understanding American politics or, quite the contrary, could it mean that there is a particular constitutional formulation of the public interest that has proved sufficiently durable and adaptable so that it does not operate as a salient feature of political events in America? In effect, Americans have not sidestepped the classical problem of the collective good, but rather, discovered a unique resolution of it. This interpretation would involve a rejection of David Truman's position that we need not account for an all-inclusive interest because one does not exist and of Glendon Schubert's position that there is no operational standard against which to judge official behavior. In fact, there is an empirical standard—the existing authority structure—and an analytical standard—what will generate the most satisfactory consequences. The rejection of the public interest concept thus appears closely allied to the study of those political events that operate within an acceptance of the given authority structure, yet this rejection becomes quite problematic when looking at political phenomena that attempt to challenge, transcend, readjust, or reinterpret this structure through political appeals and political action. The lack of a public interest theory may help explain why there is a tendency to avoid explaining such phenomena in political terms and such an interest in seeking out sociological and psychological answers for this "deviancy."[6]

Beyond the American example, we encounter the essentially Hobbesian position that the end of politics need not be seen in any terms aside from the terms of stability and public order. In Hobbes's view, it was quite enough to consider the state as a vehicle—through centralized power—for establishing and preserving a stable setting in which individuals could pursue their private wants without destroying one another. Today such a position may be translated into.

terms such as systems maintenance, equilibrium, etc. We ought now to be in a position to appreciate why it is not at all clear or satisfactory to conceive of political ends in this way. Pragmatically, the fact of stability or of a well-maintained system is related to the facts about the quality of that stable, maintained situation. The very point of the present analysis is that the goal of stability is not exclusive of, but in fact dependent upon, an effective, authoritative, and operative conception of the public interest. Indeed, a bit of reflection suggests that it is rather difficult to imagine what the exclusive goal of stability would even mean concretely. How do we imagine stable order being created without any reference to people's wants and/or needs concerning their quality of life seen both personally and collectively? Hobbes's real point, therefore, was not that stability is the only end, but that given the condition of man, as he saw it, the secure pursuit of private desires and the creation of a public condition free of criminal disorder was a more than satisfactory conception of the public interest. That, of course, is open to historical and theoretical revision.

In attempting to identify some analytical implications of a theory of the public interest, the largest of all is the effect it has on our conception of the very nature of politics. In this sense, the value of the approach taken here is that it identifies the uniqueness of man's political experience as contrasted with other aspects of social life. Among other things, it may suggest to us the possibility of more serious and precise uses of the adjective "political," as in political alienation, political modernization, political freedom, etc. All such uses may take on a more distinctive significance if we understand the generic idea of politics. The distinctiveness of politics derives from the distinctiveness of the human dilemma to which it is a response— the determination of the public interest. Therefore, politics is not simply a kind of decision-making, but the making of decisions about decisions; if the associational life of man in various spheres—religious, educational, cultural, economic—is thought of as the first order of his social life (the household!), politics is the second order, above the rest. The study of politics can, in fact, be seen as the study of a people's active consciousness of themselves. Being in its purest form such a reflective act about such consequential matters, it is not at all surprising that so much thought about politics has gone awry because of apprehensions and fears. On one count, it is perhaps the student of politics who must be the most wary of succumbing to such apprehensions, not because his error need be so consequential but because it is so easy and tempting. It is easy and tempting to reduce our political theories to the more comforting currency of economic models, power analysis, determined human ends, or positivistic epistemology. Yet the ultimate political question to which such comforting approaches are at best groping and searching steps is the question of what kind of collective future a society is going to have. Whether we feel secure or not about the notion of a public interest, such a collective future condition is the essential consequence of man's political acts. And to try to understand politics without reference to such consequences, as objects for collective appraisal, ethical judgment, and action, can only lead to an increase in a sense of frustration and inefficacy, if not a feeling of the tragic and absurd.

NOTES

1. See Thomas Kuhn.
2. John Schaar, pp. 892–893.
3. Schaar, p. 893.
4. Aristotle, *Politics*, p. 72.
5. Aristotle, p. 286.
6. See John Bunzel, Daniel Boorstin, and Lewis Froman.

BIBLIOGRAPHY

Arendt, Hannah. *Between Past and Future.* New York, 1954.
————. *The Human Condition.* New York, 1958.
Aristotle. *Nicomachean Ethics,* trans. M. Oswald. New York, 1962.
————. *Politics,* ed. and trans. Ernest Barker. New York, 1962.
Barry, Brian. "Justice and the Common Good," in *Political Philosophy,* ed. Anthony Quinton. New York, 1967.
Baskin, Darryl. "American Pluralism: Theory, Practice and Ideology," *Journal of Politics,* XXXII, 1 (February, 1970).
Berlin, Isaiah. *Four Essays on Liberty.* New York, 1969.
————. "Machiavelli," *The New York Review of Books,* XVII, 7 (November, 1971).
Bone, Hugh, and Austin Ranney. *Politics and Voters.* New York, 1963.
Boorstin, Daniel. *The Genius of American Politics.* Chicago, 1953.
Brecht, Arnold. *Political Theory: The Foundations of Twentieth Century Political Thought.* Princeton, 1959.
Bunzel, John. *Anti-Politics in America.* New York, 1969.
Burks, A. W. "Peirce's Conception of Logic as a Normative Science," *Philosophical Review,* LII (March, 1943).
Cnudde, Charles, and Deane Neubauer, eds. *Ecpirical Democratic Theory.* New York, 1969.
Connolly, William E., ed. *The Bias of Pluralism.* New York, 1969.
Dahl, Robert. *Modern Political Analysis.* Englewood Cliffs, New Jersey, 1963.
de Chardin, Teilhard. *The Phenomenon of Man.* New York, 1959.
de Jouvenel, Bertrand. *Sovereignty.* Chicago, 1957.
de Tocqueville, Alexis. *Democracy in America.* 2 vols. New York, 1945.
Dewey, John. *Characters and Events,* ed. Joseph Ratner. New York, 1929.
————. *Essays in Experimental Logic.* New York, 1960.
————. "Existence of the World as a Problem," *Philosophical Review,* XXIV, 4 (July, 1915).
————. *Experience and Nature.* New York, 1958.
————. *Freedom and Culture.* New York, 1963.
————. *Human Nature and Conduct.* New York, 1930.

———. *Individualism: Old and New.* New York, 1962.
———. *The Influence of Darwin on Philosophy.* Bloomington, Indiana, 1965.
———. *Liberalism and Social Action.* New York, 1963.
———. "Liberating the Social Scientist," *Commentary,* IV (October, 1947).
———. *On Experience, Nature and Freedom.* Indianapolis, Indiana, 1960.
———. *Philosophy and Civilization.* New York, 1963.
———. *Philosophy, Psychology, and Social Practice,* ed. Joseph Ratner. New York, 1963.
———. *The Public and Its Problems.* Denver, Colorado, 1960.
———. *The Quest for Certainty.* New York, 1960.
———. *Reconstruction in Philosophy.* Boston, Mass., 1957.
East, J. P. "Pragmatism and Behavioralism," *Western Political Quarterly,* XII (December, 1968).
Easton, David. *The Political System.* New York, 1971.
Edelman, Murray. *The Symbolic Uses of Politics.* Chicago, 1967.
Elliot, William Y. *The Pragmatic Revolt in Politics.* New York, 1928.
Flathman, Richard. *The Public Interest.* New York, 1966.
Friedrich, Carl, ed. *Nomos V: The Public Interest.* New York, 1962.
Frohock, Fred M. *The Nature of Political Inquiry.* Homewood, Illinois, 1967.
Froman, Lewis. *People and Politics.* Englewood Cliffs, New Jersey, 1962.
Gunn, J. A. W. "Jeremy Bentham and the Public Interest," *Canadian Journal of Political Science,* I, 4 (December, 1968).
Haas, Michael, and Henry S. Kariel, eds. *Approaches to the Study of Political Science.* Scranton, Pennsylvania, 1970.
Haworth, Lawrence. "The Experimental Society: Dewey and Jordan," *Ethics,* LXXI (October, 1960).
Hayek, Friedrich. *The Road to Serfdom.* Chicago, 1944.
Held, Virginia. *The Public Interest and Individual Interests.* New York, 1970.
Hennessy, Bernard. *Public Opinion.* Belmont, California, 1965.
Holmes, Robert L. "John Dewey's Moral Philosophy in Contemporary Perspective," *Review of Metaphysics,* XX (September, 1966).
Hook, Sidney. "Pragmatism and Existentialism," *Antioch Review,* XIX (Summer, 1959).
Horton, John. "The Dehumanization of Alienation and Anomie," *British Journal of Sociology* (December, 1964).
Jacobson, Norman. "Political Science and Political Education," *American Political Science Review,* LVII, 3 (September, 1963).
James, William. *Essays in Radical Empiricism.* New York, 1958.
———. *The Meaning of Truth.* Ann Arbor, Michigan, 1970.
———. *A Pluralist Universe.* New York, 1909.
———. *Pragmatism.* New York, 1955.
———. *The Principles of Psychology.* 2 vols. New York, 1950.
———. *The Varieties of Religious Experience.* New York, 1961.
———. *The Will to Believe.* New York, 1956.
Kaplan, Abraham. *The Conduct of Inquiry.* San Francisco, California, 1964.
Koch, Adrienne. "Pragmatic Wisdom and the American Enlightenment," *William and Mary Quarterly,* XVIII (July, 1961).
Krislow, Samuel. "What Is an Interest? The Rival Answers of Bentley, Pound and McIver," *The Western Political Quarterly,* XVI, 4 (December, 1963).
Kuhn, Thomas. *The Structure of Scientific Revolutions.* Chicago, 1962.
Lasswell, Harold. *The Future of Political Science.* New York, 1963.
———. *Psychopathology and Politics.* New York, 1960.

Latham, Earl. "The Group Basis of Politics," *American Political Science Review*, XLVI, 2 (1952).

Lenin, V. I. *What Is to Be Done?* New York, 1943.

Machiavelli, Niccolo. *The Prince* and *The Discourses*. New York, 1950.

Marcuse, Herbert. *One-Dimensional Man*. Boston, Mass., 1964.

Maritain, Jacques. *Man and the State*. Chicago, 1961.

McCoy, Charles, and Playford, John. *Apolitical Politics*. New York, 1967.

McLuhan, Marshall. *Understanding Media*. New York, 1964.

Metz, J. G. "Democracy and the Scientific Method in the Philosophy of John Dewey," *Review of Politics*, XXXI, 2 (April, 1969).

Miller, D. S. "James' Doctrine of the 'Right to Believe,'" *Philosophical Review*, LI, 6 (November, 1942).

Mills, C. Wright. *Sociological Imagination*. New York, 1959.

Mosca, Gaetano. *The Ruling Class*. New York, 1939.

Murphee, I. "Peirce: The Experimental Nature of Belief," *Journal of Philosophy*, LX, 12 (June, 1963).

Murphy, A. E. "John Dewey and American Liberalism," *Journal of Philosophy*, LVII, 13 (June, 1960).

Nisbet, Robert A. *The Quest for Community*. New York, 1969.

Odegard, Peter. "A Group Basis of Politics: A New Name for an Ancient Myth," *Western Political Quarterly*, XI (September, 1958).

Ortega y Gasset, José. *The Revolt of the Masses*. New York, 1932.

Peirce, Charles S. *Chance, Love and Logic*, ed. Morris Cohen. New York, 1968.

_____. *Collected Papers of Charles Sanders Peirce*, ed. Charles Hartshorne and Paul Weiss. Cambridge, Mass., 1931.

_____. *Philosophical Writings of Peirce*, ed. Justus Buchler. New York, 1955.

Plato. *Republic*, trans. F. M. Cornford. New York, 1945.

Riesman, David. *The Lonely Crowd*. New Haven, Connecticut, 1950.

Roelofs, Mark. *The Language of Modern Politics*. Homewood, Illinois, 1967.

Rorty, R. "Pragmatism, Categories and Language," *Philosophical Review*, LXX (April, 1961).

Rousseau, Jean-Jacques. "The Social Contract," *The Social Contract*, ed. Ernest Barker, New York, 1962.

Royce, J. *The Philosophy of Loyalty*. New York, 1936.

_____. *William James and Other Essays On the Philosophy of Life*. New York, 1911.

_____. *The World and the Individual*. New York, 1959.

Rytina, John Huber, and Charles P. Loomis, "Marxist Dialectic and Pragmatism: Power as Knowledge," *American Sociological Review*, XXXV, 2 (April, 1970).

Sabine, G. H. "Pragmatic Approach to Politics," *American Political Science Review*, XXIV (November, 1930).

Sartori, Giovanni. *Democratic Theory*. New York, 1965.

Schaar, John. "Some Ways of Thinking about Equality," *The Journal of Politics*, XXVI (1964).

Schattschneider, E. E. "Political Parties and the Public Interest," *Annals of the American Academy of Political and Social Science*, CCVIII (March, 1952).

Schlaretzki, W. E. "Scientific Reasoning and *Summum Bonum*," *Philosophical Science*, XXVII, 1 (January, 1960).

Schubert, Glendon. *The Public Interest*. Glencoe, Illinois, 1960.

Schumpeter, Joseph. *Capitalism, Socialism and Democracy*. New York, 1942.

Slochower, H. "John Dewey: Philosopher of the Possible," *Sewanee Review*, LII (January. 1944).

Smith, D. G. "Pragmatism and the Group Theory of Politics," *American Political Science Review*, LVIII, 3 (September, 1964).

Smith, J. W. "Pragmatism, Realism and Positivism in the United States," *Mind*, LXI, 242 (April, 1952).

Sorauf, Frank. "The Public Interest Reconsidered," *The Journal of Politics*, XVI (November, 1957).

Strout, Cushing. "Pragmatism in Retrospect: The Legacy of James and Dewey," *Virginia Quarterly Review*, XXXXIII (Winter, 1967).

Thompson, Kirk. "Constitutional Theory and Political Action," *Journal of Politics*, XXXI, 3 (August, 1969).

Thorson, T. L. *The Logic of Democracy*. New York, 1962.

Toulmin, Stephen. *Foresight and Understanding*. New York, 1961.

Truman, David. *The Governmental Process*. New York, 1951.

White, H. B. "Political Faith of John Dewey," *Journal of Politics*, XX, 2 (May, 1958).

White, Morton. *Social Thought in America*. Boston, Mass., 1957.

Wilkins, B. T. "James, Dewey and Hegelian Idealism," *Journal of Historical Ideas*, XVII, 3 (June, 1956).

Wilson, James O., and Edward Banfield. "Public-Regardingness as a Value Premise in Voting Behavior," *American Political Science Review*, LVIII, 4 (December, 1964).

Wolff, Robert Paul. *In Defense of Anarchism*. New York, 1970.

_____. *The Poverty of Liberalism*. New York, 1968.

Wolfinger, Raymond E., and John Osgood Field. "Political Ethos and the Structure of City Government," *American Political Science Review*, LX, 2 (June, 1966).

Wolin, Sheldon S. "Political Theory as a Vocation," *American Political Science Review*, LXIII, 4 (December, 1969).

INDEX